THE WORLD *Mythology* SERIES

Fabled Cities,
Princes & Jinn
from
Arab
Myths and Legends

FABLED CITIES, PRINCES & JINN

from

ARAB MYTHS and LEGENDS

TEXT BY KHAIRAT AL-SALEH
ILLUSTRATIONS BY RASHAD N. SALIM

PETER BEDRICK BOOKS
NEW YORK

Peter Bedrick Books
2112 Broadway
New York, NY 10023

Published by agreement with Eurobook Ltd, England

Library of Congress Cataloging-in-Publication Data
Al-Saleh, Khairat.
    Fabled cities, princes & jinn from Arab myths and legends / text by
Khairat Al-Saleh ; illustrations by Rashad N. Salim.
        p. cm. – (The World mythology series)
    Includes bibliographical references (p.   ) and index.
    ISBN 0-87226-924-8
    1. Arabs – Folklore. 2. Folklore – Arab countries. I. Title.
II. Title: Fabled cities, princes, & jinn from Arab myths and
legends. III. Series.
GR268.A73A4 1995
398.2'0917'4927 – dc20   94-38256
                                                          CIP

Printed in Italy by
Grafiche Editoriali Padane, Cremona
5 4 3 2 1 95 96 97 98 99

THE AUTHOR

Khairat Al-Saleh was born in Jerusalem and spent her early
years in Damascus. She graduated from Cairo University
and later did her M.A. degree in English dramatic literature
at the University College of Swansea. She has lived in
Britain since 1970 and is a poet and painter who specializes
in illumination and Arabic calligraphy. She has published
many articles and took part in writing an extensive course
for teaching Arabic to English-speaking students.

THE ARTISTS

Rashad Salim is an Iraqi, born in Khartoum and brought up
among a family of artists. He spent his childhood in several
countries including China and Sweden, then graduated
in 1980 from the Institute of Fine Arts, Baghdad. He was
a member of the Tigris Reedboat expedition, following
ancient trade routes and now works as a freelance artist.

The line drawings are by Peter Dennis.

Contents

The Arabs and their world

The lands of ancient Arabia lay in the Arabian Peninsula, stretching from the Indian Ocean in the south to ancient Palestine, Syria and Mesopotamia in the north. Throughout history the nomadic tribes of Semitic peoples who inhabited the Syrian desert and the steppe lands around the edges of the Peninsula filtered into the area known as the Fertile Crescent, the semi-circle curving from Palestine to the Persian Gulf. The earliest known established settlement in Mesopotamia, the land between the rivers Tigris and Euphrates, was that of Sumer which flourished some 6000 years ago. However, these fertile lands were soon overrun by the Semitic people, the Akkadians in the third millenium BC. Successive waves of Semitic peoples followed, the Amorites, who were known as the Canaanites in south Syria and as the Phoenicians in the north, the Assyrians and the Babylonians, the Aramaeans and the Hebrews. But while in the eastern Mediterranean Greek civilization grew to its peak and the Assyrians and Babylonians fought for dominance, the Arab Peninsula passed through the final thousand years BC in semi-isolation. Its vast deserts formed a protective barrier against invaders while the powerful defences of the great empires beyond its boundaries prevented the Arabs from expanding their territory.

Thus Arabia, no longer able to share in the major events of world history, was thrown on its own resources. Its peoples were divided into two main groups which, although closely related, were made quite distinct by the different geographical and social environments in which they lived. The Arabs of the South were the peoples of the city kingdoms of Ma'īn, Saba, Qatabān, Hadramaut and Zofār, and lived in the south western part of Arabia (Yemen and Hadramaut). The people of the North lived in Hijāz, Najd and Yamāma and were in turn divided into two groups: the nomads of the steppes who led a harsh meagre life, and the settled people of the oases and caravan cities which sprang up along the trade route, the famous Incense Road of antiquity.

The Arabs of the South or Yemenites are also known as the Sabaeans after their greatest kingdom, or as the Himyarites after their last kingdom of Himyar. They created a powerful and wealthy state whose fabulous riches inspired the writers of classical times to mix fact and fiction in the records they left of the land they called Arabia Felix (Arabia the Fortunate) or Arabia Odifera (Perfumed Arabia). The Sabaeans were ruled by priest kings who carried the title of Mukarribs and wielded both temporal and religious powers. They worshipped the sun, the moon and the evening and morning stars. The moon deity 'Ilmaqa was associated by early Arab archaeologists with the famous Queen Balqīs (The Queen of Sheba) whose ruined temple with its tall columns and monoliths could be seen emerging from the rubble and sand dunes which still cover the greater part of Arabia's history.

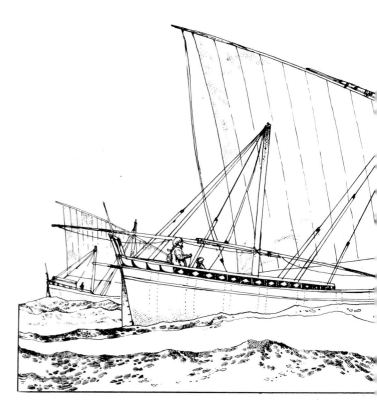

Sabaean civilization was soundly based on agriculture and trade, and as well as the great temples and many-storeyed palaces its people built, they devised and constructed what in many historians' opinion was the greatest dam ever built in ancient times. Intended to irrigate the fields and groves of Ma'rib, the great commercial capital of the ancient world, the Dyke of Ma'rib was lovingly and religiously maintained by the Sabaean kings for almost 1500 years from the date of its erection around 875 BC until its final collapse, probably in AD 600. It is believed that the height of the dam was over 8m; its solid embankment towered above the Wadi Udhana, extending between two massive retaining stone towers each about 17m high. The dam held back seasonal flood water from the hills, releasing it through a system of sluices, sediment basins and a network of canals into a number of main canals, then into 25 lesser channels each with its own holding walls.

This engineering and irrigation feat was only surpassed by Saba's tremendous commercial and maritime successes which spanned nearly 3500 years; for the peoples of Arabia Felix manned and serviced the Incense Road, the most important highway of the ancient world, from the time of Sumer to the fall of the Roman Empire. The incense tree was mainly cultivated in the groves of Hadramaut and the Sabaean colonies of Socotra and Somalia and its crops of myrrh and frankincense were among the goods most in demand in the ancient world. The cultivation of the tree was surrounded in mystery; Herodotus wrote about 'winged serpents guarding the incense groves' of Yemen and a chosen group of men tending them who were not permitted to touch women.

The cultivation of incense was not the only secret the Sabaeans jealously guarded for they also managed to keep secret their discovery and subsequent mastery of the monsoon winds which enabled them to assume an almost complete monopoly of the sea trade with India and China. The legend of Arabia Felix grew and spread more widely still, since it was now believed to produce not only incense but all the aromatics and luxury goods which they imported from the east. From India they brought sandalwood, ebony, spices, silk and precious stones; from Africa ivory, horn, slaves, cinnamon and aromatics. And to the Near East and India they carried cloth and clothing, aromatics, incense, glass and metalwork, weapons and tools, wine and grain. The network of trade routes they established consisted of sea routes which connected Ma'rib with the Indian Ocean, the Horn of Africa and the Red Sea ports, and overland routes which connected it with the Fertile Crescent across the Arabian Peninsula.

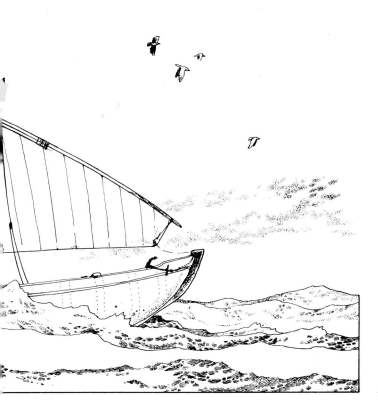

The nomadic north Arabians, perpetually seeking water and grazing grounds for their animals, were too mobile and too harrassed by their ruthless environment to be able to establish a permanent stable social order. With the exception of the great trading city kingdoms of Petra, Hatra, and Palmyra, which established settled communities, the north Arabians continued their scattered existence, owing allegiance to no state but only to their tribes. Without them, however, their more prosperous neighbours in the south could not have maintained their supremacy for it was the north Arabians who domesticated both the camel and the horse.

By domesticating the camel, the nomads were able to survive the cruelties of desert life. They sailed the seas of sands on their camels, the ships of the desert, just as their neighbours sailed the oceans in their efficient ships. The south Arabians with their superior military strength, were able to control the nomads and so harness to their service these two vital animals. An important part of their trade route was overland and without the help of the nomad's camel and later his sleek, swift horse, south Arabian trade

could not have been carried and guarded so successfully as it passed through the harsh desert country and its caravan cities of Najrān, Mecca, Gaza, Petra, Palmyra and Hīra.

In order to maintain their prosperity, the south Arabians had to remain in strict control of the Red Sea and the straits of Hormuz and Aden, their route to the Indian Ocean. However, the Ptolemies, who were building Egypt into a major naval power, eventually began to challenge the Sabaeans' commercial supremacy. When, towards the second century BC they succeeded in discovering the secret of the monsoons, they were able to establish a direct route between India and Egypt and their discovery marked the turning point in the history of Arabia Felix. Its gradual decline was accelerated by other foreign powers who were fighting for supremacy in the Near East: the Parthians and the Seleucids, the Parthians and the Romans and lastly the Sassanids and the Byzantines. As the country distintegrated into warring feudal states, a new agent, religion, created more divisions. Judaism, Christianity and Zoroastrianism all fought to secure a foothold in Yemen and to uproot each other. Finally, in the sixth century AD, the Abyssinians, then the Persians conquered Yemen and brought its long period of political independence to an end.

The decline of Arabia Felix and the rise and fall of the Arabian trade kingdoms in the Fertile Crescent all took place during what the Muslim Arabs labelled the 'days of wildness' or *Al-Jāhiliyya*, the pagan pre-Islamic era. It was towards the end of this uncertain time that Arabian poetry appeared with astonishing suddenness, perhaps brought to life by the undercurrents of unrest and the undefined, almost hidden aspirations which swept the Arabian Peninsula on the eve of the birth of Islam. Even the earliest examples of classical Arabic poetry show outstanding metrical subtlety and a verbal richness unique in the history of Arabic literature. Besides functioning as the register or *dīwān* of the Arabs, poetry gave them a sense of history and belonging and a kind of imaginative unity in the absence of a political one. The oldest examples of classical Arabic poetry date from around 130 years before the emigration of the Prophet Muhammad from Mecca. Many of the poems and odes that survive from this period glorify the deeds of the warlords of Ayyām Al-'Arab, as the battles the tribes fought amongst themselves were called.

The Arabian poet was regarded as one gifted with knowledge beyond ordinary humans and as his function developed, he began to assume many roles including that of leader, spokesman, soothsayer, teacher, chronicler and priest. Many poets were accomplished horsemen and hunters who rode in search of adventure and helped to establish a code of chivalry based on noble deeds and acts of bravery, loyalty and self-sacrifice. This code, epitomized by the word *murū'a,* gave the wild, undisciplined nomads a glimpse of a more heroic and idealistic way of life, thus paving the way for Islam and for Muhammad's divine message. An Arab historian summed up the character of the pagan Arabian like this: 'The Arabian in general and the Bedouin in particular is a born democrat. He meets with his sheikh on an equal footing. The society in which he lives levels everything down...But the Arabian is also aristocratic...He looks upon himself as the consummate pattern of creation. To him the Arabian nation is the noblest of all nations...In the purity of his blood, his eloquence and poetry, his sword and horse and above all in his noble ancestry, the Arabian takes infinite pride. He often traces his lineage back to Adam.'

The birth of Muhammad (about AD 570) and the coming of Islam, heralded not only a revolutionary change in Arabia but an upheaval that was to affect the whole known world. Muhammad's tribe, the Quaraysh, were the ruling tribe of Mecca, which had been established for some generations before Muhammad's birth as the centre of political and religious life in pagan Arabia. Muhammad's call for the worship of the one God ('there is no God but God') was greeted by his tribe with great hostility. His emphasis on godliness and a religious way of life based on charity, equality and neighbourly love rather than on blood and tribal ties roused the apprehensions of the Quaraysh, the Lords of Mecca, and they eventually succeeded in driving him and his followers out of his birthplace.

The Prophet and his followers emigrated in AD 622 to Yathrib, north of Mecca and later called Medina, where he had been invited to preach his message in peace. This emigration marks the beginning of the Islamic era and the first Islamic century. The Prophet established a religious community in Medina but the energy of the new religion was not to be confined and before long Islam's great expansion had begun. Before his death, Muhammad had conquered Mecca and its pagan idols, and taken control of the Arabian Peninsula. He died unexpectedly in Medina in AD 632 and his death was followed by a struggle for leadership among his followers. The four Orthodox Caliphs who were elected to succeed him managed for some time to keep control of the different factions but after the death of the last of these, 'Ali bin Abu Tālib, Islam was split into two main sects, the Sunnis (adherers to tradition) and the Shi'ites, followers of 'Ali, the cousin of the Prophet, his son-in-law and the father of his only male descendants.

In 661 a new Caliphate or government was established by members of the house of Umayya, a clan of the tribe of Quaraysh. They founded a hereditary monarchy and under them the seat of government was transferred from Arabia to Damascus. Another branch of the Prophet's family, the 'Abbāsids, overcame the Umayyads in 749 and established their own dynasty in Iraq, where they built their new capital of Baghdad, the scene of many of the *Arabian Nights* tales. However, an Umayyad prince managed to escape and founded a new dynasty in North Africa and Spain in the second half of the eighth century.

By the beginning of the eighth century the great wave of Arab conquests and expansion had reached its furthest limits. In less than a century half of the known civilized world was under the new religious and cultural rule of Islam, from Spain to the boundaries of China with both the Persian and Byzantine empires conquered, with Syria, Egypt, Iraq and Persia converted to Islam and with Muslim armies advancing through the Balkans and Afghanistan. The reign of Harūn Al-Rashīd (786-809) marked the Golden Age of the 'Abbāsid Caliphate and the height of Arab supremacy in the empire. But after his death the fragmentation of the vast Arab empire began and numerous dynasties sprang into existence.

The seventh and eighth centuries also marked the Golden Age of Arab geography which lasted until the eleventh century. The legendary seven voyages of Sindbad the Sailor show the restless spirit of adventure and the pioneering drive which had made the pagan Arabs of the past cross the menacing deserts and unknown seas and which now prompted them to sail the oceans of their new world with the same courage, patience and endurance. Arab ships, sailing off the coasts of China and Zanzibar, succeeded in establishing the greatest network of sea routes the world had ever known, to be matched only hundreds of years later by the great European geographical explorations.

Whereas poetry had given the Arabs a sense of pride and history, Islam gave them a sense of destiny and brought them face to face with a spiritual and religious experience which, applying equally to all people, gave them a unity of purpose. It enabled them to construct a system by which they could interpret life on earth and man's destiny and place in the universe. Islam inspired the Arabs with a universal vision which enabled them to spread the word of God beyond their own boundaries. With its intrinsic respect for knowledge and learning, and its emphasis on exploration and search for enlightenment, Islam made it possible for the culturally inferior Arabians to absorb the colourful civilizations of the classical world they now overran and to contain and preserve them within their new civilization. A distinctive world culture emerged, maturing with remarkable swiftness, with the Arabs at its very centre.

In addition to Islam, perhaps the most valuable contribution which the Arabs brought to their new world was their language. Despite the fact that Arabic had proved itself an excellent language for poetry and religion, confronted with the superior cultures and rich literatures of the ancient world, it might have been gradually replaced if it had not been for the fact that the Arabs loved and took great pride in their language and that it was the language of the Holy Koran. With its flexibility, rich vocabulary and ability to form new words, it soon proved more than a match for Greek, Syriac and Persian and became the principal medium of expression for the new world culture. Arabs and non-Arabs used it as a vehicle for literature, philosophy, philology, theology, medicine and mathematics. The Arab's love for the word showed itself in the evolution of an intricately imaginative script whose variety and floral and geometrical elaborations made it ideal for the decoration of both great monuments and fine manuscripts and whose elegant proportions helped to turn it into a high form of art.

The myths and legends in this book are divided into two main sections, the old myths of pre-Islamic Arabia and the folk tales and legends of the Golden Age of the Arab Muslim world. In some of the early stories such as the Creation and the Fall of Man you will find similarities to the accounts in the Bible, for the Hebrews were also Semitic people and shared many of the same basic beliefs. The stories in the second part reflect not only the overwhelming influence of Islam but also the vitality and imagination of the people who were once the rulers of the world.

Gods of the ancient Arabs

To believers in Islam, the city of Mecca in Saudi Arabia is the most holy place in all the world for it was there that the Prophet Muhammad was born. It is towards Mecca that the devout turn at their daily prayers, and to make a pilgrimage to Mecca is the goal of all true followers of the Prophet.

The first historian to mention Mecca was the Greek Ptolemy who referred to it in the second century as Macoraba, a flourishing trade centre in Arabia; but the story of Mecca begins thousands of years earlier. Long before the coming of Islam and long before records began Mecca was considered to be a holy place. It was here that the first House of God (the Ka'ba) was built, raised by Ādam himself, the father of mankind, according to a heavenly prototype.

The myths and legends concerning Mecca and every other aspect of Arabian life, customs, manners and religious beliefs in pre-Islamic times, were written down in the early epochs of Islam. Before Islam, legends and tales were passed on orally; they were the property of all the wandering tribes, who spread them in the same way as pre-Islamic poetry was spread, with incredible speed and amazing thoroughness. When the parables and stories were collected by scholars and linguists under the patronage of the early Muslim rulers, some of them were given new interpretations, influenced by Islamic beliefs and traditions and by the many cultures absorbed by Arabic Islamic civilization. A great number of them, however, retained much of their Bedouin characteristics of stark directness and a simplicity which often hid a deeper meaning.

The story of Mecca given here, and the part played by both Ādam and the prophet Ibrāhīm in the building of the Ka'ba, is derived from three sources: pre-Islamic myths and religious beliefs; the Koran, the sacred book of Islam; and Islamic folklore, which added many colourful details and descriptions to the basic account in the Koran.

It is believed that when God created the earth, the very first part He shaped was the sacred area around Mecca. Then He laid the rest of the earth out around it so that Mecca occupied the very centre of the world and was the navel of the earth, the mother of all cities. After God had completed the creation of the earth and heavens, the sun, the moon and the stars, He made the angels from light. Then He made the jinn from smokeless fire. He ordered the jinn to inhabit the earth while He commanded the angels to circle the Sacred House which stood just below God's throne, to praise and worship Him in heaven.

Next, God planned to create Ādam, a man who would be His viceroy over the new world He had made. At first the angels objected for they feared that Ādam would spoil the world and defile it with the shedding of blood. God was angered by the angels' protests and, to regain His favour, they built on earth an imitation of God's Sacred House in heaven. This, they said would be a refuge for the new human race, a place where humans could shelter from the wrath of God and seek forgiveness for their sins. The angels themselves worshipped God there, circling the earthly House of God, the Ka'ba, as they did their own heavenly one.

God created Ādam from dry clay and moulded him from black loam, breathing His spirit into him to give him life. He ordered the angels to prostrate themselves before Ādam and this they all did except for one, named Iblīs (whom some regard as an angel and some of the race of the jinn).
'How can I bow to a mortal, a thing made from clay?' he asked defiantly. 'I who am made of fire, a nobler substance?'

Then God cursed Iblīs and banished him from paradise, the mansion of immortality and eternal happiness. Ādam and Hawwā, the wife God had created for him, were allowed to live in paradise in joy and serenity, free to use all the good and lovely things they found there. Only one tree and its fruit was forbidden to them by God.

Iblīs, full of hatred and resentment, stole secretly back to paradise to take revenge on Ādam and his wife. Cunningly, he tempted them to eat the fruit that God had warned them against and, in a moment of weakness, they tasted it. Because they had disobeyed him, God ordered them to leave paradise and to descend to live from that time onward on earth; there they and their descendants must live and die until the day of judgement.

Ādam, distraught and grief-stricken, begged God for forgiveness, and to console him God send down a celestial tent and ordered Ādam to erect it inside the Ka'ba. The angels who brought the tent from heaven guarded it for Ādam, protecting it against the jinns and the devils who roamed the world, and Ādam and his people worshipped God there. After many years, Ādam noticed that the original Ka'ba the angels had built was falling apart. He dug the foundations for a new, permanent House of God on the site and drew the sacred boundaries. When he died at a great age, the angels carried the tent back to heaven and the children of Ādam built a house of stone and bricks on the spot where the tent and the old Ka'ba had stood. This Ka'ba remained standing for hundreds of years, until the time of Nūh and the great flood.

As the years passed, Ādam's descendants began to forget the commands of God, so God sent the prophet Nūh, a great-grandchild of Ādam, to point out their sinful ways. It was useless; the people scorned and threatened him, taking no notice of his words. So the Lord ordered Nūh to build an ark and to take into it all those who believed in Him, with two of every living thing upon the earth. When everything was ready, Nūh climbed aboard and assigned all the humans, animals and birds he had collected to their appropriate places. No sooner were the creatures settled than the gates of heaven opened and a curtain of raging waters poured down on earth, becoming a great surging flood which drowned everything in the world.

Some said that when the flood destroyed everything on earth, the Ka'ba drifted away on the surface of the waters and was never seen again; others firmly asserted that seventy thousand angels descended to earth just before the flood engulfed Mecca and lifted the Ka'ba to heaven. They left behind only the foundations, which were surrounded by the tossing waters but never wholly submerged.

Centuries after the flood, the House of God was rebuilt by a descendant of Nūh, the prophet Ibrāhīm.

Ibrāhīm was born and spent his childhood in Babel, a city in Mesopotamia between the rivers Tigris and Euphrates. When he reached manhood, he began to attack the people of the city who were worshipping idols made of wood and stone; he tried to persuade them to return to the true religion, to worship the one and only God. One day he strode into the temple and smashed all the idols there. Angrily, the people seized him and as punishment, it was decreed that he should be burned alive. They built a great pyre and, when they had set it alight, they threw Ibrāhīm into the roaring flames. To everyone's surprise, the fire only consumed the ropes which bound Ibrāhīm's hands and feet; Ibrāhīm himself was untouched for, at God's bidding, the raging flames glowed with a cool, healing energy that brought peace to his soul.

After this, Ibrāhīm decided to leave Mesopotamia and he travelled to the lands of Canaan and Egypt. On his return he married Sārah, the daughter of the King of Harrān and settled with her in Palestine. Sārah was unable to have children and after some years she persuaded Ibrāhīm to take her Egyptian maid, Hājar, as a second wife, so that he might have a child from her.

In due course Hājar gave birth to a son, Ismā'īl, who brought great joy and happiness to both his parents. Only Sārah was unhappy. She began to regret her kindness, for jealousy tore at her heart and she could not bear to watch the young mother with her child. At last she asked her husband to take Hājar and her new-born son to the remotest place he could think of.
'I do not wish to set eyes on them ever again!' she declared.

Ibrāhīm agreed to do as she asked, sensing the will of God in all that happened to him. He made the necessary preparations for the journey, loaded two camels with water and food, and set out with Hājar and the baby. They travelled on and on, far from the places they knew, into a strange desert land. At last, weary and tired, they reached the area around Mecca, and made camp near the place where unknown to them, the Ka'ba had once stood. Only a low mound remained in the sands after the flood, covering the foundations; to the weary family it looked like just another natural dune.

The next day while they were resting, Ibrāhīm told Hājar that this was where he wanted her to live with their baby son. Hājar looked around at the arid landscape in despair. To her it looked so desolate, so forlorn: nothing but a sea of sand

stretching away endlessly, unbroken by the shade of trees or the sudden green of pasture. 'How can I stay with a helpless child in this merciless desert?' she pleaded. 'I have no friends here, no family; there is neither food nor water.' 'It is God's will,' Ibrāhīm replied sadly, 'we must bow to His wishes.'

As he left to return to his wife Sārah, Ibrāhīm prayed, entreating God to protect Hājar and Ismā'īl and to have mercy on them. 'Let thy people befriend them, O Lord. Grant them safety and the fruits of the earth so that they may worship you,' he murmured as the sand dunes rose between him and his beloved wife and son.

For a while Hājar was able to survive on the provisions of food and water which Ibrāhīm had brought but soon these were all used up and she felt the pangs of starvation and thirst begin to twist her body and her mind. Her milk dried up and could no longer feed her baby son. One morning she could endure it no longer for the baby, hungry and thirsty, had started to wail piteously, tearing the cruel silence around them with his ceaseless cries. She panicked, running aimlessly to and fro, blinded by tears and not realizing that she was tracing and retracing her steps between the mounds now known as Safā and Marwa. Seven times she ran between the two, unaware of the burning sand under her feet or of the ritual she was unconsciously performing. In future all Muslims travelling to Mecca were to re-enact the same ritual in memory of her desperate search for water.

The child missed his mother. He started to writhe violently as spasms of hunger twisted his young body, and all the time he kicked the hard stony ground under his soft feet. Suddenly the rocks below split open and the sand parted as water, pure, fresh, whispering water, gushed forth, drenching the thirsty baby, restoring him with its healing coolness. Hājar, returning at last to her senses, rushed back to find him gurgling happily as he splashed and played in the spring.

It happened that a wandering tribe, the Jurhumites, were camped not far from the place where Hājar and the baby were living. That evening they noticed large flocks of birds flying low in the distance and, knowing from experience that birds crowd to water in the desert, they made their way in the same direction. They found the birds drinking from the spring while Hājar knelt with the baby beside a newly dug well. The Jurhumites asked if they could use the water and enquired whether they could bring their tents and animals to camp around the well. Hājar gladly agreed and the tribe settled from that time as her neighbours.

From then on, the well was known as the Well of Zamzam, which means the well of abundant waters.

It was many years before Ibrāhīm returned to Mecca to visit Hājar and his son Ismā'īl, and, in obedience to the commands of God, to rebuild the Ka'ba. It happened like this. He was travelling one day in Syria when an angel appeared to him, holding the reins of the Burāq, a strange, winged, horse-like animal with the head of a man. 'Come with me,' commanded the angel, 'for God has work for you to do.'

Ibrāhīm mounted the Burāq and the angel guided him through the air. Ahead of them flew Sakīna, a serene talking wind which calmed their passage through the sky. When they were high above the earth, the angel commanded Ibrāhīm to look down and choose a site for the building of a new House of God. All the land and sea were spread out beneath him, from the barren rocky mountains to the rolling desert sands, dotted here and there with patches of green where palms and grasses grew around a bubbling well. Reining in the Burāq, Ibrāhīm hovered over the sands and pointed down. 'There!' he said firmly. 'O Friend of God, you have chosen the holy grounds of Mecca, the Sanctuary of God on earth,' cried the angel. 'Let all the heavens rejoice.'

With the sound of the angels' voices ringing in his ears, Ibrāhīm descended gently to earth again, dismounted and continued on his way.

By this time Ismā'īl had grown to manhood and had married a woman from the Jurhumite tribe. He helped his father to build the Sacred House, and when it was finally completed, the two men walked seven times around the building, praying and offering thanksgivings.

Then Ibrāhīm clambered to the top of a large rock which stood nearby. As he placed his feet on its topmost surface, he felt the rock beginning to grow taller. Higher and higher it rose until it stood out above even the highest mountain. Ibrāhīm raised his voice and called the nations of the world to prayer. Four times he called to the four corners of the earth: 'Hearken to your Lord, O people!' And from every corner of the world rose the swelling sound of a multitude of voices: 'We obey, O God, we obey.'

After the death of Ibrāhīm custody of the Sacred House passed to Ismā'īl and he in turn was succeeded by his descendants, the Hanīfs. As the years passed, however, the Jurhumites, who were stronger and more numerous than the descendants of Ismā'īl, wrenched the leadership from the Hanīfs and became rulers of the sacred territory. Gradually the Jurhumites forgot the meaning of the rituals and ceased to honour God's House. They grew proud and disobedient and began to illtreat the Hanīfs, who still kept to the religion of Ibrāhīm, worshipping the one true God. At last their behaviour became too outrageous and, in punishment, God sent a series of calamities to afflict them. The last of these was a terrible flood which overwhelmed their cities and drowned the majority of the tribe. As for the descendants of Ismā'īl, they multiplied greatly and most wandered far and wide in the world, seeking their livelihood in other lands. Some stayed in Mecca, keeping the memory of Ibrāhīm and Ismā'īl alive.

How idolatry began

One of the themes that occurs again and again in the legends of the Arabs since the oldest times is that of people forsaking the worship of God and turning to several gods or idols. The early Arab chroniclers believed that the worship of a single god in the tradition of Ādam, Nūh and Ibrāhīm was the principal religion in Arabia before idolatry was introduced; later, it was said, paganism spread widely throughout the land. No-one knows the true history of these changing beliefs but many legends were told to explain how idolatry came to take the place of Hanīffiyya, the old religion of Ibrāhīm. Several of these involve a chieftain named 'Amr, son of Luhayy and leader of the tribe of Khuzā'a.

After the destruction of the Dyke of Ma'rib, many of the people of Yemen moved northwards to new lands. The tribe of Khuzā'a, however, led by their chieftain 'Amr, decided to find a new place to settle nearer home and they advanced towards Mecca, intending to uproot the Jurhumites and gain control of the sacred territory.

'Amr was a proud and brave man, renowned for his courageous deeds and for his hospitality. His caravans, travelling between Mecca and Syria, were loaded with rich goods and by successful trading he increased his influence and power. The Jurhumites were no match for his well-trained men and he was soon able to establish himself in Mecca as Custodian and

Priest of the Sacred House. Before long he was
visited by a powerful jinnee who from that time
became his adviser and link with the spirit
world.

One day 'Amr was in Tihāma, a place near
Mecca, when the jinnee spoke to him with
unusual urgency.
'Leave Tihāma at once, for good luck and
fortune await you on your journey.'
'Without delay, O jinnee,' replied 'Amr.
'I will hurry to wherever you command.'
'Travel to the shores of Juddah,' continued the
jinnee, 'and you will find there a host of holy
idols. Bring them back with you to Mecca. Fear
nothing, fear no-one! When you have brought
them safely home, summon the Arabs to you
and proclaim,
"I bring you idols, worship them and obey."
They will do as you say.'

'Amr set out towards the shores of Juddah
and there, buried in the sands with the waves
tugging gently at them, he saw the outlines of
imposing statues. He ordered his men to dig
them out and carry them back to Mecca where

he erected them in a great circle around the Ka'ba. When it was time for the annual pilgrimage to Mecca, still obeying the jinnee's instructions he sent messengers to all corners of Arabia, summoning the tribes to come and worship the idols. Tribe by tribe they arrived, crowding the city with their people and animals, camping around the Ka'ba, worshipping the sacred idols as 'Amr commanded.

After the pilgrimage was over the tribes grew restless and started to prepare to return to their homes. 'Amr summoned their leaders and as they stood before the ring of statues, he distributed one idol to each main tribe to keep for their own and to worship. So the tribes dispersed, and idolatry spread throughout Arabia.

Another version of this legend claims that 'Amr found his idols not in Juddah but in Syria. 'Amr's caravans travelled regularly along the ancient trade route between Hijāz along the coast of the Red Sea and Syria, carrying merchandise from one place to another. Once, 'Amr decided to travel with one of his caravans and as he and his men reached the boundaries of Syria, he decided to rest in a nearby town. He dismounted and walked towards the nearest building and there he found the inhabitants congregated for worship. They were worshipping idols.

'What good are these idols?' asked 'Amr with interest.

'When we need rain,' they replied, 'we ask them for rain and they send it. When we need help we ask it from them and they give it to us.'

'Amr was impressed. 'Won't you give me one of these holy idols so that I and my people may worship it, too?' he asked.

The people thought for a moment, then agreed to give him an idol named Hubal. When 'Amr returned to Mecca he carried the idol with him and set it up in the Sacred House. Later, he obtained other idols from cities and countries he visited on his travels and erected them everywhere within the Sacred Precinct. From then on, the people of Mecca worshipped idols and forgot the religion of their forefathers.

These tales explain how the idols came to Mecca but there are others which trace their origins even further back, to a time so far in antiquity that we travel to a period just after the death of Ādam. It was thought that when Ādam died, his son Shīth buried him in a cave chamber inside the mountain of Nawdh in India. From then on the sons of Shīth used to visit this cave from time to time to honour the memory of their ancestor and to call the mercy of God upon him.

One day a descendant of Qāyīn, another son of Ādam, called his people together and spoke to them: 'O children of Qāyīn, the sons of Shīth perform a sacred ritual encircling the grave of Ādam in honour of his memory. As for us, we have no such ceremony. I am therefore going to make you an idol so that we, too, will have something to worship and honour in our own way.'

So in this legend it was the descendants of Qāyīn who became the first people to make a carved stone image and to worship it. Yet another legend explains how the idols 'Amr found came to be buried in the sands of Juddah.

Nasr, Wadd, Yagūth, Ya'ūq and Suwā' were five pious people who died within one month of each other. Their relatives were so distraught that they did not know what to do. Finally a man of the family of Qāyīn went to them and said: 'Listen, you who mourn so deeply. I cannot bring your loved ones back to life, but I can make statues which will remind you of how they looked and which will keep them forever in your minds.'

The relatives were interested so the man carved a fine statue of each dead person and positioned them where the mourning families could look at them and find consolation. At first only the relatives were concerned with the statues and they walked around them to honour the memory of the dead. As the years passed, however, their descendants forgot the origin and purpose of the statues and began to worship them for their own sakes. By the third century after the statues had been installed, the people were saying, 'Our forefathers must have worshipped these statues because they believed they could intercede with God on their behalf. Let us honour and serve the idols and they will do us good, too.' From then on they turned more and more to the worship of the idols, forgetting to worship the true God of their fathers.

It was not until some centuries had passed that God decided to recall the people to His ways, and sent the prophet Nūh to summon them back to His worship. Nūh was the great grandson of Ādam and it was to destroy these idols and their worshippers that God send the great flood. As the waters of the flood rose and submerged the whole earth, the idols, too, were washed down, tossed violently in the waves. They drifted aimlessly for a long time until, as the waters began to recede, they were cast by the angry waves on the shores of Juddah. The idols were buried deep in the sands and there they remained hidden until the jinnee of 'Amr ordered the chieftain to take them back to Mecca.

Sacred animals

Many ancient peoples practised animal worship and the ancient Arabians were no exception. Animal worship was especially well known to the Arabs of the South (the Yemenites). The creatures singled out were usually chosen because of their power to sustain life, out of fear, or in order to placate dangerous animals who might otherwise be harmful. Some tribes believed they had a kinship with the animal world. Some even derived their names from the names of animals and it was quite common to call children names such as Usāma (lion), Kulthūm (elephant), Haytham (young eagle), Aws (wolf) and 'Akrama (dove).

Most renowned of all the animal deities were the god Nasr, made in the image of a falcon, the god Yagūth, in the image of a lion and the god Ya'ūq, in the image of a horse. Other animals worshipped included the two golden gazelles of Mecca, which stood within the Sacred House. Lions were held in great awe because it was believed they were in direct contact with evil spirits: travellers approaching territories inhabited by lions, the lords of the wilderness, called upon them to grant them permission to ride away in peace.

Many of the sacred houses (places of worship built in various parts of Arabia in imitation of the Ka'ba) were called after animals, such as the House of the Wolf, the House of the Ram, the House of the Goat, and the House of the Roe. Animals also inspired the Bedouin with metaphors and images to express abstract concepts. Thus a falcon became a symbol of long life, a dog a symbol of honesty and loyalty, a fox a symbol of cunning, and a lion a symbol of courage.

Animals such as the camel and the horse, so essential to the life of both the Bedouin and the settled Arabs alike, were bound to occupy a special place of honour among creatures considered sacred. The camel was in fact the most revered of all animals, a rival even to the beloved Arabian horse, the most graceful, the proudest of the animals of the desert. The ancient Arabs studied every aspect of the camel's life, its behaviour, habits and uses, with unending interest. They knew every detail of its character and had traditional ways of attending to all the needs of this most treasured of beasts. Many camels were left to graze free and unmolested because they had been pledged to the gods or because they were she-camels which bore many young. These could neither be ridden nor killed for meat because they were held sacred by their tribe. Even their milk was forbidden to all except guests or wayfarers. To harm such camels in any way was considered an act of sacrilege.

From various scattered accounts it seems that holy camels took part in some of the sacred processions and rituals, such as encircling the House of God. They were also used to carry to the battlefield the red tents which contained the tribe's stone-gods. The red tent would be surrounded and guarded by the priestesses of the tribe and by the noble daughters of the chieftains and men would gladly die rather than see their enemies defile their holiest possessions and the honour of the tribe.

It was the custom for influential tribes to dedicate an expanse of grazing land surrounding a temple or holy object to the deity of the place. This enclosure was called *hima*, a consecrated grazing ground. It was under the direct protection of the god and no human blood could be shed upon it, no animal hunted, no bird harmed, no tree felled. *Himas* became sanctuaries for both man and beast, and anyone seeking refuge there was given unconditional protection against all his enemies. Some powerful chieftains of the desert had their own *himas*, in imitation of the gods, the boundaries of which nobody dared dispute.

One tale tells how traders from a far off land, weary of their travels, dismounted in a valley near Mecca. They baked some bread and sent one of their servants to hunt for game. The servant shot with an arrow a gazelle grazing in the *hima* of the Sacred House and carried it back to the travellers, who at once lit a fire and prepared their catch for cooking. Suddenly a great fire blazed out from under the cauldron, leaping at the men and burning them in an instant to ashes. Their clothes and goods were untouched by the flames and the three palms under which they were resting were unsinged by the heat; but those who had violated the sacred *hima* were utterly destroyed.

Sacred trees, rocks and wells

The ancient Arabs felt kinship not only with animals but also with trees, mountains and rocks. Trees growing at the edge of oases and the brooding silent crags which rose like solemn guardians in the barren, arid landscape, offered the only shade and protection to the traveller, breaking the dominance of the cruel, endless stretches of sands. They seemed to have lives of their own. It was as if they were capable of hearing, seeing and feeling, containing spirits that had the power to do good or evil and affect human life. A mountain might be looked upon as an elder brother, a tree as a sister or an indulgent aunt, and the Arabs travelled great distances to seek their blessings and to honour them. Some mountains acquired special healing powers, so the rich brought them offerings, hoping to be cured.

The most sacred tree was the date-palm and one of the most ancient of Arabian goddesses was called Nakhla (the palm tree). Palm trees

which grew in oases and along water courses were also associated with the worship of Ishtar, the Babylonian goddess of fertility and love. They were believed to have kindly influences and the spirits dwelling in such trees were referred to as *'ashīra* (close friend). The people of Najran worshipped a great palm tree whose feast they celebrated annually by offering the tree a beautiful garment which they suspended from its branches and adorned with precious jewellery. Another sacred tree was worshipped near Mecca. This was a great tree which the people decorated with weapons, shields, beads and pieces of cloth and to which they sacrificed animals. It was an act of sacrilege to cut down or burn sacred trees, especially those visited by angels or jinn. These could be identified because as people passed by, they would hear the sounds of singing and dancing coming from among their arching fronds.

However, not all trees were well disposed towards mankind; some were the homes of demons and destructive powers and these were favoured by poisonous snakes and usually bore poisonous fruits. It was wise to avoid them at all times.

The ancient Arabs also worshipped water in all its forms – as rain, storms, rainbows and most important of all, in wells. The well in the desert,

like the well of Zamzam, was a giver of life, a source of healing to men and animals alike. It restored and saved. It is hardly surprising that it became an object of worship from the earliest times.

Perhaps the most important objects worshipped by the Bedouin were stones, boulders and rocks. These held for the nomads a fascination that was unequalled by any other natural objects. To the Bedouin they were the only durable landmarks in a shifting, changing landscape. In the desert there are few objects to break the monotony of the endless sand, and the ancient Arab gazed with eager eyes at the rocks and cliffs he passed, seeing in them shapes and features reminiscent of his own, haunting faces, staring distant eyes. Whenever he found a stone unusual for its colour, shape or texture, he carried it with him, treating it with great reverence; meteorites and smooth, white stones were special favourites. The fantastically eroded rock formations and the jagged shapes of huge boulders, towering like menacing sentinels over a landscape blasted by gusts of burning wind, were considered the haunts of demons and evil jinns whose wrath was aroused by trespassers.

There were many holy mountains and hillocks, some such as Safā, Marwa and 'Arafa, within the sacred territory of Mecca. As in other parts of the world, stories were told about the mountains: in most cases it was said that they were human beings who had been turned to stone. Some had been races of giants but others were just ordinary people who had assumed these craggy shapes because of some sin they had committed, or perhaps because they were lovers, defeated warriors or evildoers fleeing from vengeance.

Sometimes the transformation was sudden and dramatic. At other times, as in the following story, it mirrors the slow changing and weathering of the rocks themselves.

A traveller once came upon two giants, a man and a woman, who lived on two neighbouring rocky mountains. The male giant spoke to the traveller in a deep rumbling voice: 'I am called Aja. I fell in love with this giantess whose name is Salma. We were driven away by our people, so we came and dwelt in these two mountains. We have lived here for five centuries until the succession of days and nights have withered us and dried up our songs.'

The traveller, awestruck by their fate, asked: 'Will you permit me to stay here with you and offer you the comfort of my companionship?'

The two giants nodded slowly and the man made his camp at their feet. In years to come travellers who went that way noticed nothing but three mountains, leaning towards each other as if sharing a secret not meant for human ears.

The Arabs of the desert were fascinated with the idea of *maskh*, the transformation from human shape into the likeness of an animal, tree, or stone. Sometimes a whole tribe was thought to be capable of shape-changing. The people of a tribe of southern Arabia for instance, were said to transform themselves into wolves in times of severe drought. After feeding like animals on anything they could scavenge, they would change back into human shape by rolling about in the sands. Another tribe, the Bani Sakhr (children of rock) were believed to be the descendants of a mountain near Madā'in Sālīh in the north. With such traditions it was easy for the pagan Arabs to believe also that animals such as dogs and rabbits were the offspring of ancient peoples who had suffered the misfortune of changing their shape.

The major gods

As well as worshipping idols and the spirits found in animals, plants, rocks and water, the ancient Arabs believed in several major gods and goddesses whom they considered to hold supreme power over all earthly things. The most famous of these were Al-lāt, Al-'Uzza, Manāt and Hubal. The first three were thought to be the daughters of Allah (God) and their intercessions on behalf of their worshippers were therefore of great significance. Al-lāt, Al-'Uzza and another deity, Al-Zuhara, often shared each other's attributes, so that the status and powers of one were often transferred to another. In addition, they took upon themselves the roles of some of the lesser gods, thus increasing their stature even more.

Al-lāt, also known as Alīlat, was worshipped in the shape of a square white stone. She was known to other Semitic people in Syria and Mesopotamia, and was the Mother Goddess of Palmyra (in northern Syria), whose symbol was the lion. The Nabataeans of south Jordan and south Palestine worshipped her as the sun goddess, the giver of life. In Mecca, Al-lāt had a *haram* (sanctuary) and a *hima* where the Arabs flocked to perform the rites of worship and sacrifice which would bring her favour upon them.

Al-'Uzza was worshipped in the form of three palm trees, a stone and an idol. She was the supreme deity of the tribe of Quraysh, the rulers of Mecca immediately before Islam. She had a temple and a *hima* there and was offered gifts in gold and silver and adorned with jewellery. Her name means 'the most cherished' but she was a cruel goddess who could be appeased only by the shedding of blood, both human and animal. Like Al-lāt, Al-'Uzza was associated with the goddess of love, Al-Zuhara, but was more closely linked with Al-lāt. The two were often worshipped together and sometimes formed a trinity with Manāt or the god Hubal. Replicas of them were carried by the clans of Quraysh when they went to war to inspire the fighters with courage and devotion.

Al-lāt and Al-'Uzza were destroyed by the Prophet Muhammad after his victory over the tribe of Quraysh. It was told that when Khālid, the great Muslim hero, went to demolish the temple of Al-'Uzza, he started by felling the three palm trees sacred to her. As he struck the last of them with his sword, a black she-demon with dishevelled hair suddenly appeared, threatening him and baring her teeth. The priest who served in her temple rushed to her aid but Khālid was too strong for them and killed both demon and priest. Then he smashed her image into pieces and reduced her temple to ruins so that her power was destroyed for ever.

Manāt stood on the sea-shore between Mecca and Medina. She was worshipped in the shape of a black stone and referred to as the daughter of God, but was also regarded as the god of death and fate. The name Manāt is derived from the Arabic words *maniyya* and *manūn*, which mean death, destiny, time. The concept of man's fate on earth, the transience of life, its changes and its treacheries, caught the imagination of the Bedouin and became one of the most common themes in old Arabic poetry. No wonder that Manāt, the goddess of death and fate, was one of the most ancient gods of Arabia.

Hubal was associated with the Semitic god Ba'l and with Adonis or Tammuz, the gods of spring, fertility, agriculture and plenty. His cult was introduced by 'Amr, the son of Luhayy, who is said to have brought the great idol to Mecca. Hubal's idol used to stand by the holy well inside the Sacred House. It was made of red sapphire but had a broken arm until the tribe of Quraysh, who considered him one of their major gods, made him a replacement in solid gold.

Wadd, another ancient god, was worshipped in the image of a stately man, wearing a long garment and a wrapper, with a sword at his waist and a bow on his shoulder. In one hand he carried a lance and a standard, in the other a quiver full of arrows. Some say he resembled the Greek god Eros, and his name in Arabic means love. He was associated with the Babylonian tree of love and with the Yemenite god of the moon. He was worshipped throughout Arabia but seems to have come originally from the tribe of 'Udhra, famous for its poet lovers, who in their lives, deaths and poetry embodied the ideals of platonic love and fidelity.

The stars

The sun, moon and stars were the calendar of
the Arab nomads, who regulated their daily lives
by the rising and setting of the stars and the
changing aspects of the moon. They believed
that rain, wind, heat and cold were governed by
the movements of certain stars and they observed
and described them with great accuracy.

Al-Zuhara, the morning and evening star, in
the form of a beautiful woman, was in turn a
winter goddess, a goddess of fertility and the
daughter of God. She also acted as the goddess
of women and of marriage, and was often linked
with Al-'Uzza and Al-lāt, other daughters of
God. The animals sacred to her were the dove
and the gazelle. She symbolized beauty,
happiness, singing, dancing and frivolity and she
presided over all matters related to love. As
queen of heaven the sight of her would bring
consolation to lovers, and joy to all.

One of the most interesting legends about Al-
Zuhara involves two angels, Harūt and Marūt
and takes place some time after the death of
Ādam, when mankind had become so sinful that
the angels were outraged and despised the
humans for their weakness and frivolity. God
decided to test the angels, to see how they would

manage in the same circumstances. He ordered
them to choose two of the most learned and
pious of their number. When Harūt and Marūt
had been selected, God gave them the feelings
and desires of human beings and sent them
down to earth to live like men. Only, He
commanded, 'You must not drink, worship an
idol or lust after a human being.'

Soon after they came to earth, they met a
beautiful woman, Al-Zuhara, who was as fair as
the heavenly stars themselves. They longed for
her love but she said,
'I will only yield to you if you worship the idols
of my people.'

The angels refused to sin against God and Al-
Zuhara went away. A few days later they
returned to her house and again pleaded with her
for her favours.
'I will consent to all you ask if you promise to
do one of three things: worship an idol, kill a
man or drink wine.'
'Never,' said the two angels, turning sadly away.
Yet again they returned to seek her out and this
time they were so overcome with desire that
they agreed to drink wine with her. As they lay
drunkenly enjoying themselves they saw they
were being watched by another man and, fearing
that he would betray them, they killed him.

The angels in heaven were astonished at what
had happened to their brothers, the best and
strongest of their number. And realizing that the
lives of humans were more difficult than they
had thought, they took pity on them and prayed
to God to forgive them their sins.

As for Al-Zuhara, she had learned from the
two angels the secret words required to ascend
to heaven and as soon as she was alone, she
uttered them and was lifted high into the sky
where she wandered among the stars. When she
was tired of exploring, and wanted to return to
earth, she found that she had forgotten the
words that would take her down. So God
transformed her into a star, fixing her to the roof
of the sky, where she remains until the end of
time.

In addition to the sun, moon and the star Al-
Zuhara, the Arabs worshipped the planets
Saturn, Mercury and Jupiter, the stars Sirius and
Canopus and the constellations of Orion, Ursa

Major and Minor and the seven Pleiades.

Some stars and planets were given human characters. According to legend, Al-Dabarān, one of the stars in the Hyades group, fell deeply in love with Al-Thurayya, the fairest of the Pleiades stars. With the approval of the Moon, he asked for her hand in marriage. Al-Thurayya objected, saying coquettishly, 'What would I do with a fellow like that, with no money?'

Al-Dabarān decided to find a dowry worthy of her and he collected some beautiful young camels to present to her. He returned, driving the camels before him, determined to persuade her to marry him. It was not to be. The red star 'Ayūq stepped between them to obstruct his path and there, fixed in the heavens, he has remained ever since. Still today on a clear night you can see the three stars: Al-Thurayya leading the way with 'Ayūq and Al-Dabarān followed by his herd of stars forever pursuing her across the sky.

Rites and pilgrimages

The annual pilgrimage to Mecca was the greatest religious festival of the pagan Arabs. It was a unique opportunity for the tribes from far and near to flock together and experience for a few months the unity and brotherhood which they could not otherwise achieve. The political and social structure of the tribes, with its great emphasis on the ties of blood relationship and the importance of an individual's undivided loyalty to his clan, normally kept them very much apart but during the sacred months in which the pilgrimage took place, fighting and the shedding of blood in revenge were taboo. On the way to Mecca, the travellers would break their weary journeys at a series of oasis fairs where they could rest and drink, water their animals, listen to the singing girls, exchange goods and renew their supplies.

The most famous of these oasis fairs was held at 'Ukāz, a valley between Mecca and Medina. This was not only an important social and commercial event, but was the poetry festival of the ancient Arabs, a fair where poets competed to display their talents and vied with each other in excellence and eloquence. The warrior poets of the desert recited their stirring odes to spell-bound audiences who listened with attention verging on awe to the recital of adventures and heroic deeds, the praise of beautiful women and the swiftness or nobility of the poet's horse. The poets competed for the highest honour that could be bestowed on a living person, for the winner was awarded a unique prize: his poem, inscribed in golden letters, was suspended on the walls of the Sacred House in Mecca. Seven such poems found their way to the walls of the holy Ka'ba, thus gaining immortality. They were called the Mu'allaqāt, the Suspended Odes, and are still considered to be the greatest masterpieces of Arabic poetry.

After the fair, the journey no longer seemed so long and difficult and the pilgrims who had feasted on poetry set off refreshed, drawn onwards by the promise of Mecca. Once arrived at Mecca, the ceremonies started with a ritual walk around the Sacred House, followed by a walk to 'Arafa, the holiest of the sacred hills of Mecca. There the pilgrims congregated in reverence, preparing for the next ritual, the sacrifice.

The offering of sacrificial animals to the gods was perhaps the most important ritual of all for the pagan Arabs. The flesh was usually eaten by the hungry pilgrims, or thrown for birds and domestic animals to feed on; the gods demanded only the blood as their share. After the slaughter, blood was poured over the idols and the holy stones and god and worshipper shared in the sacrifice. The blood appeased the deity while the meat eaten by the worshippers signified the union between god, man and his offering.

The rites of worship always included a ritual walk around the image of the god and other holy objects. As they circled or danced reverently the worshippers chanted and clapped, repeating the phrase, 'We obey you Lord, we obey,' over and over again. The pilgrimage ended with a last ritual walk between the sacred hills of Safā and Marwa – the same hills between which Hājar the wife of Ibrāhīm, had paced in her frantic search for water. Finally, the pilgrims cut or shaved their hair and prepared to leave the holy city.

The soul and life after death

The pagan Arabs did not have a clear and definite idea about what life was like after death, but they seem to have believed in the survival of the soul after the death of the body. At the moment of death, it was said, the soul left the body in the shape of a fluttering bird (*hāma*) which, distressed and forlorn, hovered over the corpse, crying piteously for its owner.

Birds like this were often encountered in desolate places, in graveyards or where someone had met a violent death. Some of the soul-birds, however, flocked near the homes of children of the dead, in order to inform them of what had happened to their parents. The soul-bird was believed to take the shape of an owl, sometimes an eagle. It emerged from the skull as a tiny bird but as time went on became a strong, full-fledged bird. If the dead person had been murdered, his soul-bird would haunt the spot where the crime had taken place, clamouring 'Quench my thirst, quench my thirst!' Nothing but the blood of the killer, shed in revenge, would appease the bird and still his cries.

Many stories were told about the uncanny power of the soul-bird and its dramatic flights. One relates how Layla Al-'Akhyaliyya, a famous Arabian poetess, fell in love with a fellow poet from her tribe named Tawba. Their families did not approve of the match so Tawba, grief-stricken, wrote this poem:
Should Layla pass by my grave and greet me
Through rock and stone I shall return her
* greeting.*
My soul will fly to her, a fluttering, crying bird.

Soon afterwards, Tawba died and Layla was married to a man of whom her family approved. Her husband, however, knew that his wife had loved Tawba and he watched her jealously, hardly letting her out of his sight. Years later, the couple were travelling when they passed the grave where Tawba lay. The jealous husband, remembering Tawba's poem, turned to Layla, 'Dismount! I order you to greet Tawba in his grave!'

Weeping uncontrollably, Layla refused but he ordered her again to do as he wished. Reluctantly, Layla dismounted and approached the grave, tears streaming down her face.
'Peace be with you, Tawba,' she said brokenly.

She had hardly finished speaking when a bird like a white dove shot out of the grave, flew towards her, then circled up into the sky and vanished. Terrified, she clutched her breast, screaming. Then she fell on Tawba's grave, her fingers gripping the cold stones. When her husband reached her to help her up, it was too late; she was dead.

Another story shows a less frightening aspect of life after death. The life and deeds of a man named Hātim are shown in Arabic literature as the embodiment of the ideals of generosity and hospitality. People believed that even after his death his grave sheltered the hungry and offered a refuge to the fugitive: it became a *hima*, a sanctuary for wayfarers and wanderers in need of protection.

Once a traveller passed by Hātim's grave on his way to visit friends. As he approached the tomb, he noticed a huge cauldron leaning against it, just like the ones Hātim had always used for entertaining his guests when he was alive. On each side of the grave he saw four maidens, leaning forward as if they were weeping for the grave's owner. With their hair streaming over their shoulders, the maidens looked so beautiful, so graceful, that he stood still for a long time feasting his eyes on their beauty.

Later he was told that the maidens were placed there by jinns to guard the tomb while Hātim looked after his guests at night as generously as he had ever done in the past. In the daytime a traveller might be lured towards the grave by the beautiful figures that looked like maidens only to find himself staring at four shapely stones. But at night, as soon as it was dark, the maidens would gradually emerge from the stones, accompanied by their guardian jinns. Then they would dance around the tomb and begin their nightly keening, lamenting Hātim's death, he who was the most generous of Arabs.

Myths and legends of the extinct Arabs

The early Muslim historians, following the traditions of the old Arabian genealogists, worked out some very interesting and complicated family chains of descent which traced back the origin of all the ancient Arabians to Ādam. Tribes memorized their family trees painstakingly; they became part of the tribal lore, treasured by the sages of the tribes and passed down by word of mouth from generation to generation.

Ancient historians divided the Arabs into two groups: the 'extinct' Arabs who were the oldest inhabitants of Arabia and the 'extant' or existing Arabs. According to old records the extinct Arabs were believed to have perished almost without trace either because God had punished them for their sins or because they had destroyed one another in warfare. These were the legendary peoples of Thamūd, Tasm, Jadīs, the Jurhumites, and 'Ād who were descended directly from Ādam through his son, Shīth, and grandson, Iram. It is the stories of these ancient peoples that are told in this chapter. The first is the story of Thamūd and the prophet Sālih.

There was once a race of people who possessed the rare gift of longevity. They lived in Al-Hijr, between Hijāz, along the Red Sea coast, and Shām (Syria) and were called the Thamūdites. They lived for such a long time that their houses fell into ruins long before they themselves died, so they searched for a way in which to make their homes more durable.

It so happened that Al-Hijr was surrounded by rocky mountains and it was these mountains that eventually provided the answer to the Thamūdites' problems. They built a lofty city out of the solid mountain rock, cutting and carving great chambers with smooth, polished walls, digging deep into the mountainside. Then, to adorn their new homes, they added pinnacles, friezes and pillars of intricately worked stone, making houses and palaces that would last for ever.

The people of Thamūd were filled with admiration for their rocky city. But their self-satisfaction turned to conceit. They sinned and grew oblivious to God. So the Lord sent the Prophet Sālih to remind them of their duty to God and to bring them back to His true religion.

Only a few people responded to Sālih and listened to the word of

God. Most took no notice of his advice. One day Sālih went to a feast held by the Thamūdites in honour of their deities and idols so that he could point out to them the uselessness of their gods. They listened indifferently as they had always done in the past, but this time said to Sālih, mockingly, 'If what you say is true, ask your God to prove it by showing us a miracle. Let this mighty Lord of yours command a camel to come out of that great rock. She must be a camel to surpass all others: a milch camel, with soft, white wool, a noble animal of pure blood who will give birth to many others like her.'

Sālih agreed but he, in turn, had conditions to lay down. 'It shall be as you wish, but once the camel appears at God's bidding no-one must ride her; she must not be hurt in any way and you must always see that she is allowed to graze and drink as much as she wants.'

The people agreed and Sālih and his people went to the rock to wait. Nothing happened for a few moments and the tension mounted. Then suddenly the rock began to moan like a woman about to give birth. It was seized with convulsions like the contractions of labour, shaking the earth with its struggles. Then, after a last great effort, the rock gave birth to a camel so great in size that she resembled the mountains around her: each leg alone measured one hundred and fifty metres; her width was seventy metres and the length from her hump to the tip of her tail, seven hundred metres. The camel of God stood on unsteady legs in front of Sālih, light streaming from her eyes and from her pearl-studded harness. Dazzled, the people of Thamūd stood staring at her, too stunned to move or speak.

The camel was already pregnant and, before the people could recover from their shock, she in turn gave birth to a calf. Then she made her way to the top of the mountain, the calf at her heels. Every morning as the sacred camel came down from her high mountain pasture to offer the Thamūdites her milk, she would call to them in a clear, high-pitched voice in their own tongue, 'He who wishes to drink my milk, let him come forth.'

Since the sacred camel needed a large amount of water, it was decided that she and the Thamūdites would use the water supply on alternate days. This and the fact that the camel offered free milk to everybody made the Thamūdites grumble, especially those with large herds who could no longer sell their milk.

Two women from Thamūd, one beautiful and rich, the other elderly with four pretty daughters, decided that something must be done. The first woman went to a strong young man, a relative of hers, and promised to give herself to him if he killed the camel. The second woman followed her example by promising one of her daughters to another young man. These two men in turn incited others against Sālih and the camel until there were seven more conspirators.

The next day, as dawn was breaking, the nine men lay in wait for the sacred camel to come down the mountain with her calf. As she appeared in the ghostly morning light, they leaped out at her and attacked her with swords and arrows, cutting her legs and shooting arrows through her udder. Her calf managed to escape unharmed; he fled to the top of the mountain, lowing piteously for his mother.

It was not long before Sālih heard the bad news. He wept for the camel of God and then he turned to his people and said to them sadly, 'You have committed an evil deed. Follow the camel's calf and at least comfort him, so that the Lord may have mercy on you and lessen your punishment.'

Filled with foreboding, the Thamūdites went with Sālih to find the calf. As they began to climb up the mountain after him, they felt the earth tremble and it began to rise higher and higher at God's bidding, until the top of the mountain touched the clouds. When the calf saw Sālih approaching in the distance he wept until the fur of his face was soaked in tears; then he cried out three times with a heart-rending sound and disppeared inside the rock. Sālih turned to his people and said, 'You have three days before the judgement of God falls upon you. On the first day your faces will turn yellow, on the second day they will turn to the colour of blood and on the third, they will turn black as tar.'

Everything happened as Sālih had predicted. On the first, second and third days, the Thamūdites wailed and trembled in anticipation of the disaster that was coming, as their faces

turned first yellow, then red, then black. When the fourth day came the earth shook with a noise like thunder, splitting the smooth polished walls of the rocky palaces, toppling the mighty stone pillars and crushing the delicate stonework into a thousand fragments. Next morning the earth was still but the people of Thamūd lay dead, trapped in the ruins of their city. Only Sālih and his followers were spared. They were taken away from their devastated homes by an angel of God who guided them to new lands far away.

The woman with the wonderful sight

Tasm and Jadīs were sister tribes that lived in Yamāma near Bahrain. A Tasm chieftain called 'Amlīq seized power over both tribes. He was a cruel and unjust ruler; he tyrannized the tribe of Jadīs and they lived in fear of him.

One day a woman from Jadīs and her husband went to see 'Amlīq about a quarrel they had had over a boy slave. In mockery of all notions of justice, the chieftain ordered the couple to be sold and the boy to join his own slaves. The woman expressed her anger by composing a poem about 'Amlīq in which she ridiculed him and attacked his injustice. The poem spread quickly by word of mouth and soon everybody was repeating it. Eventually it was brought to 'Amlīq's attention. He was exceedingly angry and decided to punish the whole tribe of Jadīs. He decreed that no bride should go to her husband on her wedding night without first coming to him.

There was nothing the people of Jadīs could do but to suffer this humiliation in silence until the proud Shamūs, the sister of the ruler of Jadīs was married. On her wedding night 'Amlīq claimed her. She resisted but he overcame her. Weeping with rage and shame, Shamūs ran from the room calling to the men of Jadīs, 'Shame on you people of Jadīs, shame on you. Your men are even weaker than your women.'

Still overcome with anger at her humiliation, she composed and recited an angry poem describing the degradation her people were forced to suffer in silence. Provoked by her words and the dishonour of his house, her brother at last decided to act. Since he was under constant surveillance he had to resort to treachery. He invited 'Amlīq and all his retainers to a great banquet in his pavilion. When all the guests had sat down at the table and food and drink had been laid before them, he and his men snatched up the swords they had conveniently buried under the rugs that covered the sand and killed 'Amlīq and most of his men.

The few that survived the attack managed to escape to Himyar in Yemen. There they sought refuge with King Hassān. This king decided to help the Tasm tribe by marching at the head of a great army against their enemies, the Jadīs. As they approached the lands of the people of Jadīs, one of the kings's men came up to him and said, 'I have a sister who is married to a man from Jadīs. She has the gift of long sight; her eyes are so sharp that she can pick out a man thirty miles away. She is called Zarqā Al-Yamāma, the blue-eyed woman. You must beware of her, for no Arab has keener sight than she.'

When he heard this, the king ordered his men to cut down all the trees they could find, to tear off their branches and to advance to Jadīs hiding behind them. The army was still within a day's march of the land of Jadīs when Zarqā, who held the office of priestess, saw them coming with her keen eyesight.

'I see trees marching,' she called in warning. 'But look, I see a man devouring the shoulder of an animal behind one of the trees. Now I see more trees advancing. No, I see more and more men, with branches growing from their heads and limbs. Prepare yourselves for war, for how can trees and men march together?'

The people of Jadīs only laughed at her, refusing to believe her strange warning. When dawn came the next day, the enemy army attacked and killed all the men; the women and children they took as captives. But Zarqā, whom the king regarded as a dangerous witch, was killed cruelly at the gates of the city. Curious to discover the secret of her amazing eyesight, he ordered her eyes to be examined by his wisest physicians. The only unusual thing they found was that they were stained and smudged with

thousand and two hundred years. During his lifetime he married one thousand women and fathered four thousand children. While he reigned, his kingdom prospered and was peaceful, for he was generous, charitable and just; and he ruled over a people renowned for their prudence and might.

Like their great ancestor, the later 'Ādites were a nation of giants. The shortest among them would have towered over the tallest of our trees. They were so large that their heads looked like great domes; eagles and hawks built their nests in their nostrils and in the corners of their eyes. When they walked the earth shook. When they talked the clouds trembled.

As the centuries passed, the 'Ādites, in their lofty palaces and well-built towers, forgot the teachings of Nūh and the worship of God. They misused their great strength and behaved unfairly towards their weaker neighbours. Power corrupted them and in their conceit they believed that no harm could ever come to them. The 'Ādites put all their faith in three idols: Sada, Samūda and Hiba. These they believed would protect them against the consequences of their evil deeds and the sins they committed so freely.

Then God chose a good and pious man from among them and asked him to preach to his people, to show them the extent of their wicked ways and to bring them back to God again. This man was named Hūd and was the great grandchild of 'Ād, the founder of the nation. Some 'Ādites listened but most showered him with ridicule.

'Why should we listen to this fellow?' they said. 'Who can harm us? Nowhere in the wide world is there a nation as mighty and as prosperous as ours.'

God saw that the 'Ādites were unmoved by Hūd's words so he decided to give them a harsher warning. He withheld the rains from the land of 'Ād for thirty years. A great drought afflicted the land: the wells and springs of the oases and the green valleys dried up; crops withered in the fierce heat of the sun and both men and animals died of hunger and thirst.

The 'Ādites did not know what to do. Eventually they decided to send a deputation to

black powder—for Zarqā was the first Arab woman to use kohl, the fine black powder now used all over the world as eye make-up. From that day onwards, the women adorned themselves with kohl and the land of Jadīs became known as Yamāma, in memory of Zarqā Al-Yamāma, who tried to save her tribe.

The vengeance of God

'Ād was a nation of giants who were believed to be the descendants of Sām, the son of Nūh. They were mighty in strength and enormous in stature, a prosperous, industrious people, who lived in al-Ahkāf, between Oman and Hadramaut in Southern Arabia, where they built great, soaring cities and palaces.

The founder of this nation, also known as 'Ād, was the great-great grandchild of Sām. 'Ād was colossal, as tall as a mountain and as sturdy. He worshipped the moon and lived for two

Mecca for, although they had forsaken the worship of God, they knew that Mecca was the most holy of places and that it was there, if anywhere, that they would obtain help. At that time, Mecca was the home of another race of giants, called the ʿAmālikites. Their lord was himself an ʿĀdite on his mother's side so the deputation was welcomed warmly and their arrival celebrated with feasting and singing.

The ʿĀdites had come to pray for rain but it was not long before they forgot the purpose of their visit and spent their time with two beautiful slave singers in the Lord of Mecca's household. As the weeks passed, the Lord of Mecca began to be concerned. He knew the hardships his mother's people were suffering and felt responsible for the unfeeling behaviour of his guests. To remind the deputation discreetly of their neglected mission, he ordered the two slave girls to sing a poem lamenting the fate of ʿĀd. The two girls sang of the terrible thirst that spared neither man, woman nor child; of the hunger that weakened them so much that they had no strength to raise their voices to frighten

away wild animals which now roamed the land fearlessly, straying in and out of their homes in full daylight.

As they listened, the 'Ādites were overwhelmed by grief and remorse. Without losing any more time they rushed into the sanctuary of the House of God to pray, begging God for his forgiveness. Only Lukmān, one of 'Ād's youngest sons, did not go with them; he it seems had a reason of his own for coming with the deputation.

The leader of the mission knelt to pray for rain and he had hardly finished speaking before a deep voice broke like thunder through the clouds, calling to him: 'Behold, God has made three clouds: one white, one red, and one black. Choose one of these clouds, choose your fate and the fate of your people.'

Looking upwards, the 'Ādites saw the three clouds, one white, one red and one black, hovering above their heads, as if waiting for their decision. Their leader thought for a moment and then chose the black cloud. 'For it is the harbinger of rain,' he said, 'the forerunner of plenty.'

As they watched, the black cloud drew apart from the other two clouds and, blown by a strong wind, was carried through the sky towards Southern Arabia.

Far away, in the land of 'Ād, the people saw the cloud approaching in the distance, a mass of swirling blackness, its edges torn and tattered by the speed of its movement through the air. 'It is rain,' they cried thankfully, 'our punishment is over at last. The rains are coming.'

Only one 'Ādite, a priestess named Mahdad, gazed at the cloud with wide, wild eyes for she saw the fate that awaited her people in its menacing, advancing shape. She gave a cry of fear and fell to the ground, her body writhing and twisting in uncontrollable convulsions. When at last she came to her senses she called to the people of 'Ād, 'Why do you rejoice? That frowning cloud is the cloud of vengeance. It is the curse of 'Ād. I can see within it the winds of death, being driven onwards by strange and monstrous figures.'

As she spoke, the earth shuddered and the winds broke loose, sweeping and roaring across the parched land. For seven nights and eight days the gales raged, uprooting and ravaging everything in their path. Men and camels were blown away like insects; like grains of sand, the stones of palaces and houses were scattered in the storm and like feathers floating in the wind great trees were uprooted and carried upwards.

Some tried to escape: they rushed to hide in caves in the giant cliffs, or took shelter behind great rocks, crawling into holes and under boulders. But wherever they hid, the relentless wind hunted them down, picking them up with tongues of fire, then hurling them into the air or down into the abyss. Those who escaped the curse of the winds met an even more terrible fate. Huge, black birds appeared from the raging, tumultuous sky. Swooping down to earth, the birds of vengeance snatched the people up in their beaks and talons and carried them to the sea, where they dropped them down into the hissing, boiling waves.

So the nation of 'Ād came to an end. All, that is, except the prophet Hūd and his followers, whom God protected from his angry wind. When the wind died down on the eighth day, only this small company of holy people were left in a landscape strewn with the dead, who lay outstretched on the ground like the trunks and branches of giant palm trees.

Lukmān and the seven falcons

Lukmān, the son of 'Ād, had refused to join the deputation of the 'Ādites who prayed for rain in the Sacred House. Instead he knelt some distance away from them and prayed to God with a request that was for himself alone. 'O God, lord of the emerald seas and of the green oases,' he prayed, 'I implore you to grant me the gift of long life, that I may live longer than any man has lived before.'

'Your wish is granted,' replied a voice from heaven, 'but although you will live for many, many years, you may not become immortal. Choose which life span you will have—the lives of seven generations of dark mountain gazelles or the lives of seven generations of powerful

falcons. Choose wisely, O son of 'Ād.'

Lukmān thought for a moment. He thought little of the lifespan of seven gazelles, so he chose that of the falcons. Then he left the Sacred House and set off by himself.

One day, when he was climbing a high mountain, he heard a voice in the distance calling to him, 'O Lukmān, son of 'Ād, who believes that falcons will live forever, come here, to the top of the mountain, and discover for yourself that man cannot escape what is written.'

Lukmān did as he was told and there, at the top of a high crag, he found a falcon's nest containing two chicks. He picked up the stronger of the two and carried it in his arms all the way back to his camp. The little falcon became his constant companion for Lukmān brought it up with care and love, feeding it on the best scraps of meat from his own meal, carrying it always on his wrist and teaching it to soar up into the clear air after its prey and to return obediently at his command. The young falcon grew into a proud, strong bird, devoted to its master, feeding from his hand alone and never leaving its side.

For eighty years the falcon was Lukmān's faithful servant. The day came, however, when the falcon found it was too weak to fly to its master to take the food from his hand. Lukmān tended it lovingly, gently stroking its drooping

head and feeding it on softened pieces of meat. Then, early one morning, the old falcon was overcome with longing for the blue skies, its wings trembled as it remembered its golden flights to the sun and it yearned to fly again. Suddenly its body shuddered in one great convulsion, then a stillness came over it and it closed its eyes forever.

Lukmān, grieving for his beloved bird, made his way back to the mountain where he had found it as a nestling. As he climbed up the crag towards the nest he felt driven by a strange force and when he at last reached the top he almost shouted for joy. There, just where the old nest had been, was another exactly the same. And there in the nest was another falcon chick fluttering its wings and gaping its beak for food. Lukmān picked it up joyously and returned to his camp where he raised his new falcon with the same care and love as he had lavished on its predecessor.

Like the first falcon, the new bird responded to Lukmān's care and remained his faithful companion for eighty years. Then it, too, met the same fate, yearning for the sky and dying in its master's hand. Four more times Lukmān returned sadly to the mountain top and four more falcons lived and died in his keeping. When he travelled to the crag for the last time to take the seventh falcon from the nest, he called it

Lubad which means 'time—the accumulation of all times' for he knew that his long lifespan, too, was nearing its end.

Eighty years passed before Lubad grew weak and old. Then, one morning the bird was unable to rise to join the morning flight of falcons. Grief-stricken and trembling with fear, Lukmān called to it, 'O Lubad, rise, for you are my eternity! Do not die, do not bring my death upon me!'

But Lubad was too weak; his wings fluttered for the last time and his eyes closed. Lukmān wept for his falcon and for himself as he knelt in terror to watch him die. When the bird was still and silent, Lukmān tried to stand but his own death was upon him and he could not rise: the seven allotted lifespans were over and he, like all men, passed at last away.

Iram of the tall columns

The lord of the 'Ādites, 'Ād, had two heirs: Shadīd and Shaddād. The two brothers ruled together over their people after their father's death until Shadīd died and then Shaddād ruled alone. He was a strong, ambitious king who never tired of conquering new lands to increase his power and established a large kingdom for himself and for his descendants.

Shaddād was also fond of learning and spent much of his time studying the lore of the ancients. As he read the old tablets and scrolls, the descriptions of paradise took hold of his imagination. He read of gold and silver palaces, decorated with pearls and sapphires, of gardens full of flowers and running streams, where the good and holy would one day live happily forever. And all the time a dream began to take shape in his imagination.

'Why can't I build an earthly paradise that would rival in glory and splendour the heavenly paradise of God?' he thought to himself. 'Why can't I, the mighty Shaddād, build the city of cities, the wonder of the world, a city that would be unique, magnificent, matchless?'

Next day, he assembled all his courtiers and noblemen and addressed them.

'Know all you gathered here that I have decided to build a fantastic city that will have no equal. It shall be named Iram of the tall columns, for its towers will pierce the clouds and its pinnacles will embrace the stars.'

The king's people listened to him in spellbound silence, not knowing how to respond. So Shaddād chose one hundred of his nobles and to each appointed one thousand men.

'Go, search for the loveliest land,' he ordered, 'find me a place where the water is clear and the air is pure and where there is plenty of space. There build me a city of gold and silver, pearl and chrysolite. Raise it on pillars of sapphire and grace it with palaces that reach for the clouds. Then, when you have done that, fill my city with perfumed gardens, rich with every kind of flower and tree. Lastly, when you have laid down my gardens and they stretch dreamily basking in the sunlight, water them with wandering rivers and running brooks, so that my paradise will resemble the heavenly paradise of God that I have read about in the records of the ancients.'

The king's nobles could foresee the difficulties that lay ahead, the kind of hardships they would have to endure to realize such a dream.

'Where can we find all this gold and silver, all these jewels and precious stones?' they objected. 'Indeed, how could we mortals build such a city anyway?'

'You know that I hold the reins of the world in my hands,' retorted Shaddād, 'therefore I bid you to write to my deputies everywhere requesting them to collect on my behalf all the gold and silver they can find. Let them send their divers to search the depths of the seas and rob them of their treasures: let their miners dig the earth for its hidden wealth of gems, onyx and turquoise. Then order them to search high and low for the rarest perfumes, ambergris, saffron, musk and aloes-wood.'

Shaddād's men searched every corner of the earth for ten years, looking for the treasures their king had commanded them to find. Those whose task it was to find the site on which to build the city found the perfect place for Shaddād's Iram near Oman: a wide open plateau surrounded by mountains, across which rivers and streams twisted and twined under clear blue skies; where the light had a strange luminous quality and the air a reviving freshness.

The architects and builders set to work at once. The architects drew a plan for a square city, the builders dug the foundations and began on the outer walls, using onyx and alabaster. Towers covered in sheets of gold and silver rose in splendour from the walls, shining so brilliantly in the burning sun that they dazzled the eyes of all who looked at them.

It took Shaddād and his men five hundred years to build the fabulous city of Iram. The tall columns which supported the palaces were each the work of many years. They were carved in a single piece, each measuring almost the full height of the mountain from which they were cut. With immense skill and effort they were transported to the site of the city, where they were erected one by one. Shaddād built one hundred thousand palaces, one for each of his chieftains and princes. Each lofty palace was supported by pillars of ruby and aquamarine. Above each elegant hall a second storey was raised, designed to surpass the first in beauty. Every room was decorated with pearls, sapphires and yellow topaz so that the light shimmered and danced in intricately reflected patterns. The floors were made of scented wood, inlaid with turquoise and pearl; even the glue the carpenters used was liquid gold mixed with richly scented musk and myrrh so that a rich, spicy perfume filled the air.

When all the buildings were completed, the river courses were dug throughout the gleaming city and orchards were planted in the gardens of the palaces. Tiny, whispering streams whose water was mixed with the perfumes of ambergris and frankincense threaded their way smoothly through the orchards. Finally Shaddād created the gardens, his long-awaited earthly paradise.

Among the sweet-scented flowers and shrubs were trees of chrysolite and jasper with leaves made of precious metals and fruit of emeralds, rubies and red hyacinth. Song birds of every kind came to live in the garden, filling the fragrant air with the sweetest songs, joining the chorus of artificial birds which sang haunting tunes as they perched in their golden cages,

fluttering their mechanical wings. Countless lamps and lanterns hung among the orchards and groves, their gleaming light competing with the sun by day and at night filling the city with flickering reflections of gold and silver and precious stones.

At last Iram was ready to receive its lord. Shaddād's dream had come true: he had built paradise on earth. He gathered together all his courtiers and servants, all his heroes and armies, and formed a huge procession. Then he marched slowly and majestically at its head towards Iram.

The golden walls burned in the sun as he approached and his heart swelled with pride. 'Surely there can be no city in heaven or earth to rival mine,' he thought. 'I am the king of kings, the mighty Shaddād. The world cannot contain my equal.'

As hints of immortality and divinity crowded into his mind, a terrible noise filled the sky, blotting out his thoughts completely. The noise lingered like a wailing cry, first all round them, then seeming to come from deep within, paralysing the nerves, freezing the blood in their veins. Then all was quite still for a fleeting moment; the fabulous city stood silent, enigmatic and empty as every living creature perished. Then suddenly the earth opened around it and Iram, bathed in a strange twilight, began to sink slowly down until the whole city was completely swallowed up. All that remained was an endless wilderness of empty, shifting sands across which the winds moaned and howled.

Iram revisited

Iram had vanished like a dream. The city of pearl and gold was never seen again except once— perhaps to serve as a reminder to mankind of his vanity. For, but for Shaddād's greed and pride, Iram might indeed have become an earthly paradise, brought to life by the laughter of children and the sounds of everyday living.

In the seventh century, during the reign of Mu'āwiyah, the first caliph of the Umayyads, a man lost his herd of camels in the wild stretches of desert in Southern Arabia. While he was out

looking for them he suddenly came across an
airy fortress within a walled city, which rose
from the sand like some giant golden eagle. He
got off his horse, took his sword in his hand and
walked towards the ghostly city. Two enormous
gates confronted him the like of which in
majesty and workmanship he had never seen
before. An unearthly light gleamed from stars of
red and yellow sapphires which decorated the
doors. He pushed the doors open and stepped
into the fabulous paradise of Iram.

After he had recovered from his surprise, the
camel-driver filled his pockets and saddle-bags
with all the treasure he was able to carry. Then
he rode to Damascus, determined to tell his

strange story to the Caliph Mu'āwiyah himself.

The caliph listened carefully to him, taking his story seriously. Then he summoned one of his old and wise retainers and asked him if he could explain the man's tale.

'O mighty king, know that this city you have heard described is the lost city of Iram of the tall columns, built by Shaddād, the son of 'Ād,' the wise man said. 'It was written in ancient records that only one man would ever enter it and that no other human eye would bear witness to its splendour until God, the Lord of heaven and earth, opens its great gates to His people at the end of all time.' Then the wise man began to tell the caliph another story of old Iram, the story of The burial chamber of Shaddād.

A man from Hadramaut once heard a tale about a certain mountain in which there was a vast cave. Mysterious things were said to happen in this cave and people were too terrified to go near it.

The man from Hadramaut, being brave and adventurous, decided to find out the truth for himself. He persuaded a young man from his village to accompany him and they set out on their journey. After a long and difficult climb up the slopes of the mountain, they came to a cave that looked out over the sea. Believing this to lead to the large inner cave they were searching for, they packed their provisions around their waists, lit a candle and prayed for the protection of God. After squeezing their way through a long narrow passage, they emerged into a great man-made chamber with smooth walls like glass. At the end of the chamber was a staircase so large that only giants could climb down it. 'Take my arm, then bend and lower me down,' the man said to his friend. 'When my feet touch the bottom of the first step, I will call up to you.' 'But what shall I do then?' asked the young man. 'When I call you, take hold of the edge of the step you are standing on with both your hands, then lower yourself down until your feet touch my shoulders. After that it will be easy.'

In this way they were able to climb down the stairs unharmed. When they reached the bottom they found themselves in yet another chamber of colossal dimensions, carved out of the solid rock and with walls as dazzlingly smooth and high as those of the last cavern. At one end stood a throne that seemed to burn with the light of countless jewels. In the dim light they could just see the form of a giant reclining on the throne. He was exquisitely clothed in many sumptuous robes, fastened by chains of gold and silver. No sound or movement came from him and the men knew that he was long dead. The chamber was lit with a mysterious, ghostly light and peering round they saw it was coming from a great tablet made of solid gold which hung suspended high above the throne. On the tablet in ancient script, was inscribed this poem:

I am the lord of Iram, Shaddād, the son of 'Ād.
The western lands I ruled and the eastern I had.
Look at me you who have heard of my might.
And know that he will perish who scorns the
   light.
Like scattered bundles of hay
In the arms of the wind we lay
As that great cry from heaven
Overtook those who could not pray.

The two men went up to the dead king and tried to remove his rich clothes but the moment their hands touched the robes they crumbled to dust, so they contented themselves with taking gold and silver chains. Then they tried to remove the precious stones from the throne but these were far too large to be carried.

All of a sudden their candle went out and the cavern was plunged in darkness. Bravely, they decided to rest and wait until the next morning before they attempted to escape from the chamber of death. Next day, after long deliberations, they decided that it was too risky to go back the way they had come. Then far away in the distance they spotted a ray of light and, hoping that this showed them a less dangerous route, they picked up all the gold and silver they could carry and pushed their way through narrow passages and long tunnels until they reached the place where the light shone through, a cave high above the sea. There they waited for three days and three nights until at last they were spotted by some fishermen and rescued.

'And from that time onwards,' said the wise man, 'the great lord Shaddād has lain silent and undisturbed.'

Myths and legends
of the North and South

The great tribes of the extinct Arabs, the legendary peoples of ʿĀd, Thamūd, Tasm and Jadīs all vanished, destroyed, it was told, by their own pride and disobedience to God and by the terrible wars they fought against one another. The surviving Arabs, known as the Extant Arabs, were divided into two groups: Arabs of the South and Arabs of the North. The South Arabians or Yemenites, lived in Yemen or Arabia Felix as it was known in the classical world. They were thought to be the descendants of Qahtān, through Sām, the son of Nūh, while the Arabs of the North were traced back to Sām and Nūh through ʿAdnān, a direct descendant of Ismaʿīl, the son of Ibrāhīm. Between the two groups lay the desert, now known as the Empty Quarter, a vast natural barrier separating North from South.

The history of Yemen is still largely undiscovered; so much of its ancient past still lies buried beneath the marble ruins of its great ancient cities. However, most archaeologists conveniently divide the history of this old country into the following periods: the mythical period; the Maʿīnite period from 1120-630 BC; the Sabaean period from about 800 BC until after the rise of Himyar; the first Himyarite period from 115 BC until AD 300; the second Himyarite period and the pre-Islamic period ending at the beginning of the seventh century.

The kingdom of Saba (known in the Bible as Sheba) enjoyed a long period of tremendous success because of its unchallenged dominance over the trade routes from India to Egypt and Syria. Between the second and third centuries AD, however, more and more trade goods came to be carried by sea, along the coast of Hadramaut, through the straits of Bab al-Mandib, and Saba's prosperity began to decline. This brought drastic changes to the settled, orderly lives of the Sabaeans, who were a community largely dependent on commerce. The decline of trade was disastrous even for those not directly connected with commerce for as people began to move away to more prosperous lands, agriculture too, was neglected.

Then, because it had been so poorly maintained, the great dam at Maʿrib started to collapse. It is now believed that the dam finally collapsed between the fifth and sixth centuries AD , but early Arab historians estimated the date to be between the first and third centuries, when, it was said, there followed a great exodus of the

Yemenite people to the north, to Hijaz, Syria and Iraq.

This one dramatic catastrophe, the bursting of the dam and the dispersing of the Yemenites, symbolizes the disintegration of Arabia Felix and epitomizes all the misfortunes of Sabaean legendary history.

Most legends tell that the Dyke of Ma'rib (the glorious capital of Saba) was built by King Saba. Other legends give the credit to either Lukmān of the seven falcons, the son of 'Ād, or to Queen Balqīs, who was helped by the jinn. The Dyke, which was made of enormous boulders cemented together with molten lead, was built between two huge mountains across the Wadi Udhana to hold back and control flood waters caused by heavy rainfall in the high mountains between Ma'rib and San'a.

The complex irrigation system devised to exploit the full potential of the dam helped to irrigate thousands of acres of desert and gradually transformed the lands of Saba into an earthly paradise. According to legend, Saba became a land of plenty with rivers and streams wandering through incense groves and cool perfumed gardens full of singing fountains and waterfalls. The people of this beautiful land grew generous and bountiful, the kings just, compassionate, and wise.

The orchards and groves of Ma'rib were so dense with fruit trees that often a woman carrying a basket on her head would find when she had passed through the trees, on her way to visit a neighbour, that her basket was brimming over with every imaginable kind of fruit. A man travelling among the trees in the meadows could walk for two months at a time without ever getting sunburned, for he was always protected by a canopy of leaves and branches.

The Sabaeans built many great palaces, the most sumptuous of which was Ghumdān, built, some claimed, for Balqīs by the jinn. Ghumdān had four facades of white, black, red and green stone and was built as a towering twenty-storey citadel. The top storey was a magnificent single chamber that had for a roof a single slab of alabaster where the king of the citadel could sit and watch the birds flying in the skies. At the four corners of the palace stood four brazen lions which roared whenever the wind blew around them. The windows of each chamber were hung with little bells, whose chiming could be heard from a great way off and, at each window, stood tall fruit trees and palms, offering their laden branches to the occupants of the palace.

One of the chief gods of the Sabaeans was the sun. They worshipped him in splendid, many-coloured marble temples and lived prosperously and peacefully under their god's protection. As the sun rose and set, so they prayed on their knees, asking for his blessing.

The two legends that follow capture two important stages in the history of the kingdom of Saba. The legend of Queen Balqīs—or the Queen of Sheba as she is known to the western world—shows Saba at the height of its glory, rich, prosperous, fabulous; the story of the queen priestess shows Saba in the twilight of decay, awaiting the final disintegration of its great civilization.

Queen Balqīs and King Sulaymān

Balqīs was the daughter of the king of Saba, Al-Hadhad, and Rawāha, the daughter of the king of the jinn.

The story of Balqīs begins early one morning long before she was born, when the king of Saba went hunting. He grew tired after a while, so he dismounted from his horse and sat down to rest in the shade of a tree. His rest was suddenly disturbed by two serpents, one white and sleek, the other black and deadly, who appeared in front of him locked in fierce combat. The king waited, watching in fascination, until the black serpent seemed to be on the verge of winning. Then he reached for a large stone and crushed the black serpent to death. The white serpent he revived with water and then allowed it to slide back into the trees.

The king returned to his palace and went to his chamber to be alone for a while. Again his rest was disturbed. This time the king was taken aback by the sight of a tall man who appeared

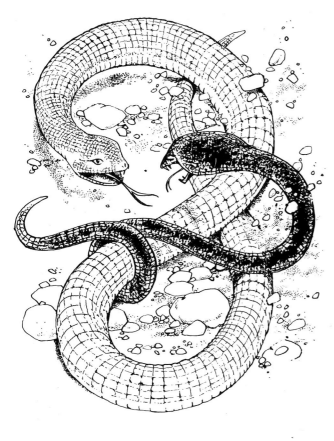

great fire burned under a cauldron. He followed her a little disturbed. Without any warning and, before he could prevent it, the queen threw the baby into the flames. The king stared at her in horror unable to believe his eyes. Just in time he remembered his promise and said nothing to her at all.

Not long afterwards he had another terrible shock. The queen gave birth to a baby girl. As before, she came out of their chamber holding the baby close to her. The king, half expecting her to go to the kitchen, made a move to block her way. Instead of walking in the queen called one of the palace dogs and threw her baby at him. Before the king could reach the baby, the dog had picked her up in its huge mouth and run off with her. Distressed beyond words, the king watched silently. He kept his promise and said nothing to the queen.

Some time later, a rebellion broke out in Saba and the king and queen set off at the head of an army to deal with the rebels. One evening when they stopped to rest in a clearing in a grove, they were greeted by a strange sight: their supplies were being rolled from their camels' backs and emptied in the dust, as though unseen hands were at work. The king knew at once what the matter was. He guessed that the invisible hands belonged to jinns who were acting on his wife's instructions. This time he could keep silent no longer, for the whole army would now starve to death. He took hold of the queen's arm and pulled her with him to a lonely place. There he stopped and called angrily, looking at the turf under his feet. 'O earth, I have suffered the sight of my son being fed to the flames and my daughter to a dog, without complaint. Now you have gone too far and we are all going to perish.' 'You would have been wiser to be patient yet a little longer,' replied the queen. 'I must tell you that your *wazir* (chief councillor) was bribed by the enemy to poison your food and water. If you had eaten or drunk any of it, you would indeed all be dead by now. However, there is a well not far from here that will give you as much fresh water as you need. As for your son, I gave him to a nursemaid to bring up for us but, alas, he has died. But your daughter, Balqīs, is still alive and well.'

from nowhere right beside his chair. 'Do not be afraid,' he said to the king gently, 'I am the white serpent whom you saved this morning from the black serpent. He was one of my slaves who rebelled against me, and had killed several members of my household. In gratitude for saving me, I offer you the gift of healing and a reward of riches.'
'I have no need of money,' said the king. 'As for the gift of healing, it is more fitting for a physician than a king. But I do have one favour to ask: if you have a daughter, do me the honour of giving her to me in marriage.'

The man agreed to the king's request on one condition. 'Whatever she does, you must not object, for if you do, she will leave you that very instant.'

The king married the jinnee princess and they lived happily until their first child, a son, was born. Hardly had the cheers and sounds of jubilation died down when the queen came out of her chamber cradling the new-born baby in her arms. The king watched as she made her way out of the great hall towards the kitchen where a

As she spoke, the earth burst open in front of them and the rocks and trees were momentarily lit up. A maiden with large dark eyes and thick, black hair reaching to her ankles stood beside them. Her father looked at her and she ran into his arms. As she did so, the queen disappeared and was never seen again.

Balqīs grew up to be a woman of incomparable beauty who was greatly loved and cherished by her father. One day, however, the king fell ill and died and Balqīs's cousin succeeded to the throne. He was a lecherous, evil man and Balqīs loathed him. It was his habit to lure all attractive young women to his chamber and then to dishonour them. Balqīs decided that something must be done about the king, so she sent him a message, offering to marry him herself. Nothing could have delighted the king more and he agreed at once. On their wedding night, Balqīs made her way to the king's palace at the head of a long procession, accompanied by her maidens and guards. When she was alone with the king, she persuaded him to drink so much that he could hardly move. When he was quite drunk, she drew her sword and beheaded him. The Sabaeans were overjoyed and invited Balqīs to become their queen, promising to honour and serve her faithfully.

The Sabaeans built Balqīs a great palace of onyx, marble and alabaster, with golden domes that reached up to the heavens. The magnificence of her burnished throne, so often celebrated in later Arab myths, was beyond belief: the crest of the canopy alone rose to a height of eighty metres; superbly carved branches climbed up its sides and back from which hung garlands of leaves and clusters of flowers, bursting open with the light of countless jewels. It glowed brilliantly like the morning sun itself.

Just as Balqīs ruled in wealth and splendour over her people in the land of Saba, so King Sulaymān, the son of Dāwūd, ruled in the land of Palestine. Sulaymān (known in the Bible as Solomon) was a wise king and a prophet of God and his reign was just and merciful. When he ascended the throne, King Sulaymān prayed to God to grant him more power than any monarch had ever had before. In response to his request, God made the jinn and demons serve him; gave him control of the winds and dominion over every beast, fish and fowl. He also gave him the gift of tongues, enabling him to speak to all living creatures.

Whenever King Sulaymān wished to travel he ordered his throne to be placed in the middle of a wooden platform that looked a little like a huge carpet. On his left and right sat his nobles, behind them sat the jinn nobility and behind them sat the demons. When everyone was seated, Sulaymān summoned his birds and ordered them to fly overhead to form a canopy of shade. Then he called the winds, commanding the strong wind to lift the carpet and the gentle wind to steer it in the right direction.

Early one morning Sulaymān and his court took up their positions on the carpet and set off on a journey to distant lands. Among the birds flying overhead was an adventurous hoopoe called Yafoor. Before long Sulaymān and his courtiers landed in a clearing to have a rest and Yafoor, taking advantage of all the activity, slipped away to explore. He flew about happily, only coming down again when he saw a beautiful orchard below him. It did not take him long to discover that he had company in the orchard for on a nearby branch he spotted a fellow hoopoe. Yafoor introduced himself and found that his friend's name was Afeer.
'Where did you come from?' asked Afeer in surprise.
'I have come from the land of Shām (Syria), with my lord Sulaymān the mighty, who is king over men, jinn, beast and fowl. But where do you come from?' asked Yafoor.
'I belong to this country, which is ruled by the great Queen Balqīs,' said Afeer proudly. 'She rules the kingdom of Saba and is the sovereign lady of ten thousand lords. If you come with me you will see just how beautiful she is.'
'I cannot be too late or my lord will miss me,' said Yafoor anxiously.

Towards noon, King Sulaymān felt the sun burning his face. He looked up to see which of his birds was neglecting his duty and saw that Yafoor's place was empty. He called for his falcon, his head bird, and demanded to know where Yafoor had gone.
'I do not know where Yafoor is,' replied the

falcon, 'for I did not send him on any errand.'

The falcon sent for the lord of the birds, the eagle, and asked him to find the hoopoe at once. The eagle flew upwards into the sky and hovered above the world looking for Yafoor. He spotted him flying from Yemen, looking very upset. The eagle swooped down onto him before Yafoor, sensing trouble, had time to speak.

'In the name of Him who made you mightier than I,' pleaded Yafoor, 'have mercy on me. Please spare me, for I have something very important to relate to my lord Sulaymān.'

Yafoor stood abjectly before the king, with bent head and drooping wings. King Sulaymān was very angry with him and scolded him fiercely, even threatening him with death.

'O mighty monarch, I have just returned from the presence of a great and beautiful queen. She has a lofty palace and a marvellous throne. But the queen and her people worship the sun,' faltered Yafoor nervously, half choking with fright.

'I will spare you this time. Go and get on with your work,' replied the king sternly.

Sulaymān decided to write a letter to the queen. In it he said, 'I call on you and your people to worship the one true God and to embrace Islam.' He ended his message by inviting the queen to pay him a visit in his country, then ordered Yafoor to take the letter to Balqīs.

The queen was alone in her room when Yafoor flew in through the open window and placed the letter in her lap. Balqīs was surprised by the letter. She thought about it for a long time but was uncertain how to reply. The next morning she assembled her court to ask their advice.

'This letter has been delivered to me. It comes from a mighty king who wishes us all to go to him and surrender ourselves to his God.'

'We are a great nation. Bid us do what is honourable and we will do it,' her chief adviser replied.

'No king has ever entered a city without ruining it,' said Balqīs.

'I suggest we send this King Sulaymān a magnificent gift. If he is a king of the world he will accept it but if, as he says, he is a messenger from God, then he will not accept the gift but insist that we follow his religion.'

Balqīs asked her treasurers to make bags of brocade and to fill them with gold and silver. Then she mounted five hundred slave boys superbly dressed and carrying the most magnificent of swords, on the most splendid Arabian stallions. On five hundred white mares rode five hundred slave girls of great beauty, dressed in silk sewn with pearls. With them the queen sent Sulaymān gifts of myrrh, frankincense and musk. Last of all, she prepared a small glass bottle in which lay a huge, unpierced pearl and a large emerald that had been pierced unevenly.

She gave the bottle to one of her wise men, asking him to deliver it personally to the king. 'Watch the king carefully,' she told the wise man. 'If he is proud and sullen, he is no man of God. If he is kind and gentle and has a pleasant manner, then he is the man he says he is.'

King Sulaymān received the long procession of the queen's messengers in his court, surrounded by a mighty host of his own men,

jinns, demons, beasts and birds. He entertained them graciously but would not accept the queen's presents.

'I have no need of riches,' he said. 'By giving me the gift of wisdom, God has made me richer than any other man in the world.'

The wise man then gave him the glass bottle and said, 'My queen wishes you to guess what is in this small bottle.'

Sulaymān was given the answer immediately by an angel.

'It contains an unpierced pearl and an unevenly pierced emerald,' he replied.

'The queen wishes you to pierce the pearl and to thread the unevenly pierced emerald,' continued the wise man. 'Can you do this?'

Sulaymān turned to his men for an answer. They had none. He consulted his jinns but they were also unable to help. So he turned to the demons. They advised him to send for the wood-fretter. The wood-fretter hurried to the king's presence and pierced the pearl quickly and efficiently. Then Sulayman asked his courtiers if there was anyone who could thread the emerald.

Not one of his men could thread the emerald but the king heard a small high voice say, 'I can, O prophet of the Lord, I can.'

Sulaymān looked down to his feet and saw a tiny worm. It took the thread in its mouth and wriggled its way through the emerald and came out the other side. The king put the pearl and the jewel back in the bottle and handed them back to the wise man.

The messengers returned to the queen taking back with them the presents that Sulaymān had refused to accept and described in detail to her all the marvels they had seen. Balqīs realized that she could not match the might of Sulaymān who, she realized had the jinn, the demons and the angels as allies. She decided to leave for his court to embrace the religion of God. Before she left, she commanded her servants to hide her throne in a palace that was built within seven other palaces. Then she herself locked the doors and posted guards in every room of every palace.

As Sulaymān watched the great procession wind its way towards his palace, led by Balqīs seated proudly on her magnificent stallion, he decided to plan a surprise for her. He had heard Yafoor, the hoopoe, mention the queen's throne, so he turned to the lords of his jinn and asked who among them could fetch the throne from Saba and place it, undamaged, in front of him.

'Before you leave this hall, it will be with you,' said one jinnee lord.

'No, I need it at once,' declared the king.

'Then it shall be with you in the twinkling of an eye,' said Āsaf, the lord of the jinn, who was a devout believer.

'So be it,' exclaimed the king.

Before any one was able to move, the floor at the foot of Sulaymān's own throne appeared to melt away and Balqīs's throne emerged. There was a gasp of astonishment as the court stared at the incredible throne.

While most of the court waited curiously for the queen's arrival, some of the jinns and demons began to discuss what was happening among themselves.

'If the king likes and marries the queen, and a son is born to them, then we shall really be in trouble,' they said. 'For if that happens we will be held in bondage as long as their descendants live. Let us tell the king, therefore, that Balqīs has donkey's legs, that she is sick and of unsound mind.'

The king listened to them but decided to see for himself if what they said was true. He ordered his jinns to build a tall palace of green glass with a floor made of a single sheet of white glass. Water was channelled underneath the floor and in the water many coloured fish and other tiny creatures of the sea swam among seaweed and sea-anemones. Lastly, Sulaymān ordered his throne to be moved into the middle of the glass floor and the queen's throne to be placed upside down in front of his.

As Balqīs walked towards Sulaymān, the fish and water creatures swimming under her feet startled her. She drew back, lifting her skirts, lest she should fall into the rushing water that seemed to be swirling around her feet in multi-coloured waves. Sulaymān looked at her bare legs: they were elegant and shapely, but, alas, they were covered with long hairs.

'Do not be afraid, gracious queen,' the king said.

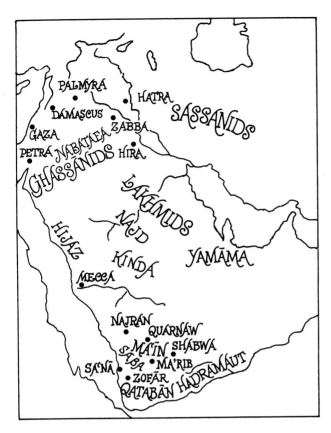

'This is only glass although it resembles water. Welcome to my kingdom.'

Then the king pointed to her throne and asked, 'Is this your throne, fair queen?'
'It looks like it,' the queen replied calmly, trying to control her surprise.

Sulaymān was satisfied with her answer for, he reflected, it indicated her healthy state of mind. If she had either denied or confirmed that it was her throne, he would have suspected her judgement. So he ordered the throne to be set upright and invited her to sit facing him. As Balqīs sat there on her throne, her beauty eclipsed all the splendours of Sulaymān's court. 'I have a riddle for you, O wise king,' she said. 'You shall have your answer, Queen Balqīs,' replied the king.
'What water belongs neither to heaven nor earth?' she asked.

The demons announced that they knew the answer and whispered it in Sulaymān's ear. 'That is easy,' said Sulaymān. 'If my horses gallop until sweat runs down their legs and if I collect this sweat in jugs, I should have water

that belongs neither to heaven nor to earth.'

The riddle answered, the king and queen relaxed in each other's company, telling each other strange stories while the jinns and demons entertained them with singing and banquets.

Some legends claim that King Sulaymān did marry the queen of Saba after the jinns had invented a substance for removing the hair from the queen's legs. But many others insist that she returned to her own country directly after she had declared her faith in one God. At home she married a king who had long been a loyal neighbour. They ruled together helped by the jinn who, on Sulaymān's instructions, built many fortresses and palaces for her and served her well until Sulaymān's death.

The queen priestess and the Dyke of Ma'rib

Once upon a time there lived a king called 'Umrān who was well versed in the lore of the ancients. Towards the end of his days, as he grew bent with age, he prophesied doom to his people and the end of their social order. 'Your cities will be deserted, your children will leave you and be scattered far and wide in the world; your way of life will come to an end, and your unity will be broken,' he told them.

'Umrān was childless and on his deathbed he summoned his brother 'Amr, the son of Muzayqiyya, and advised him to marry a priestess from his household to share his throne. 'Her name is Zarīfa,' he said. 'She will inherit all my knowledge.'

'Amr succeeded his brother to the throne and made Zarīfa his queen. One night, while she was asleep, Zarīfa felt a presence near her bed. Then she heard a voice say, 'Choose, Zarīfa! What will you have—either a child to delight your eye or knowledge to gladden your soul?'
'I choose knowledge,' she replied fearfully.

At once she felt a hand being placed on her heart as knowledge was given to her and then a hand on her womb as she was deprived of fertility.

The king and queen lived happily for a long

while, enjoying the peace and order of their kingdom. Then the priestess-queen had another dream. This dream was very different from the first one: she saw an ominous black cloud cover the land, sending down deafening thunderbolts and streaks of lightning. Shaking, her eyes wide with nameless fear, she went to tell the king of her dream.

'I have had a terrible dream', she said. 'I saw clouds burst, shedding fury and death. I saw blazing thunderbolts shatter and blast everything in the doomed world.'

The king tried to calm her. 'It is only a bad dream,' he whispered soothingly and, eager to believe him, she tried to forget her fears.

One day the king went to rest in one of his orchards with two slave girls. When Zarīfa heard where he had gone, she decided to follow him with one of her own boy slaves. As she was walking along the path leading to the orchard, she came across three rats standing on their hind legs, covering their eyes with their paws. Zarīfa knew at once that this was a bad omen and quickly crouched on the ground herself, covering her own eyes with her hands.

'Tell me the moment those rats go away,' she ordered her slave.

After a few minutes the boy told her the rats had gone, and she continued on her way to the orchard. She came to a stream and began to cross it. Suddenly a tortoise leapt out of the water in such a panic that it landed on its back. It struggled and struggled, trying to right itself, scattering lumps of earth everywhere. Zarīfa knelt beside it and watched it until it managed to return to the water. By now she was thoroughly frightened.

It was a hot and windless day and she did not reach the orchard until noon. To her consternation, the trees were swaying languidly. Growing more and more frightened, she made her way to the summer house where 'Amr was resting. 'Amr saw her arrive and assumed she had come because she was jealous. A little embarrassed, he told the slave girls to leave him and greeted his wife.

'Come in Zarīfa, come and sit down beside me.'

But the queen only stared at him and replied in a strange, trembling voice full of foreboding,

'By the bright day and the dark night, by the breath of heaven and earth, the trees will be uprooted and fall, the crops in the fields will be swept away as wave after wave of swirling water devastates the earth.'

'Who told you this?' inquired the king, disturbed.

'The rats have prophesied an age of untold sorrow. Child will kill father, brother will betray brother,' continued Zarīfa, still deep in her trance.

'I saw a tortoise digging wildly in the earth and when I came into the orchard, behold the trees were swaying but there was no breeze blowing,' Zarīfa continued, still trembling violently.

'What do you understand from these omens, Zarīfa?' asked 'Amr, beginning to be afraid.

'A terrible calamity, a dreadful disaster, woe beyond words,' moaned Zarīfa, trying to put her vision into words.

'Please explain in more detail,' begged 'Amr.

'The Dyke of Ma'rib, it is the great dyke our ancestors built that will cause this disaster', said Zarīfa.

'Amr leaped off his couch, gazing at Zarīfa in disbelief.

'What do you mean? I beg you to explain more clearly.'

'Dark sorrow, evil tomorrow, Dwindling offspring, vanishing spring,' recited Zarīfa, sinking deeper into her trance.

'How can I know that what you are saying is true? asked the king.

'Go to the dam,' said Zarīfa. 'If you see rats burrowing in the solid rock, displacing huge boulders and then pushing them down the dam, you will know that the disaster will be caused by the dyke.

The king leaped on his horse and rode swiftly to the dam and there, to his horror, he saw giant rats and red mice digging and burrowing among the rocks. As he watched, boulders too large for a hundred men to move began to roll slowly away. The truth of his wife's words began to dawn on him and he returned to the palace with a heavy heart. When he had told Zarīfa what he had seen, she said to him, 'We must leave this place and all our friends to find a new home: where rats dig, men can no longer dwell!'

'I am still not convinced', said 'Amr. 'I need some more proof that what you say will happen.'

'Sit in the orchard', replied Zarīfa, 'and order a glass jar to be placed in front of you. The orchard is well sheltered from the wind and sun, so that if the glass jar fills with sand and dust you will have your proof.'

The king did as his wife suggested and soon the bottle was full of sand and dust. Surely this was proof enough; there could be no room for doubt now, he thought.

'When will this disaster happen?' he asked Zarīfa.

'Only God knows,' she replied, 'but I will never sleep again until we have left this place.'

'Amr gathered together his household and all his family to tell them what had happened and to ask them to prepare for departure. When he had sold all his property and all his lands, he told his people also, advising them to leave. Many tribes decided to follow the king's example. They said their farewells to their lands for ever, and marched sorrowfully towards distant new homes, knowing that nowhere in the world would there be another Saba, nor a land as rich and bountiful as their home.

The Arabs of the North

In pre-Islamic times the Arabs of the North, or North Arabians as historians prefer to call them, comprised two main groups: the Arabs of Hijāz and Najd, both nomadic and settled and their kin and neighbours, the Nabataeans of Petra, the Palmyrenes, the Lakhmids, the Ghassānids and Kindites.

Petra was a key trading centre on the caravan route between Saba and the Mediterranean. Its inhabitants were an ancient people called the Nabataeans who emerged as a noticeable power towards the end of the fourth century BC in southern Jordan and southern Palestine, reaching the height of their power in the first century AD. The kings of Petra, the beautiful capital of the Nabataeans, with its splendid rock-carved chambers and temples, repeatedly challenged the authority of the growing power of Rome and as a consequence were finally conquered by Roman armies in AD 106.

Palmyra (Tadmur) was one of the greatest trade centres of the ancient world. It was situated at a junction of caravan routes which reached as far as India in the east and Rome in the west. About the middle of the third century Palmyra was caught up in the struggle between Persia and Rome for supremacy in the Near East. The merchants played Roman against Persian in their own battle to preserve their political and economic independence.

In AD 265, the Arab king of Palmyra, Udhayna, drove the Persians out of Syria earning the gratitude of the Roman Emperor Gallienus, who gave him the title of Augustus. A year later, King Udhayna was assassinated and his wife, the beautiful and accomplished Zenobia, succeeded him. Zenobia was very ambitious and wanted to built an empire for herself. She marched against the Romans, conquering the Roman-occupied countries of Syria and Egypt but, in AD 272 the

Valiant Queen of the East, as she was called, was eventually defeated by Aurelian. As time passed, the actual historical events that had led to Zenobia's defeat were forgotten by the Arabs but a legend remained in which Zenobia of Palmyra became identified with the Mesopotamian Queen Zabbā. Both were proud warrior queens and both were doomed to defeat.

The Lakhmids' history is not at all clear and is greatly mixed with legend. They are believed to have come originally from Yemen and were said to have moved north after the destruction of the Dyke of Ma'rib, once thought to have occurred at the beginning of the third century. By the end of that century they had established themselves in the north of Arabia, in Syria and Iraq, where they founded the Lakhmid dynasty at Hīra. Hīra became one of the most important Arab cultural centres in pre-Islamic times. Poets from all over Arabia came to the Lakhmid's court and their talents were handsomely rewarded. The Lakhmids became Christians and ruled their province under the eye of the Persian Sassanid kings, their neighbours, who exploited them and used their territory as a buffer between their own country and their bitter enemy the Byzantine Empire. However, relations between the Lakhmids and their Persian patrons became extremely strained as the Lakhmids began to rebel against them. Just before the coming of Islam the Lakhmids fought and won a major battle against the Persians.

The Ghassānids are also thought to have fled from Yemen after the destruction of the Dyke of Ma'rib in the third century. They, however, settled in southern Syria, Palestine, Lebanon and Damascus, where they came into contact with Greek culture. Like the Lakhmids, they adopted Christianity. Gradually they came under the power of the Byzantine emperors who recognised them as allies at about the end of the fifth century, giving their kings the titles of Phylarch and Patricius.

The Ghassānids and their neighbours, the Lakhmids, were constantly fighting over the frontiers of the two great powers, the Romans and the Persians, whom they were compelled to serve. Ghassānid culture, which was a mixture of Arab, Greek and Byzantine was more sophisticated than the Lakhmids' but they were alike in never completely submitting to their great neighbours. Indeed, Al-Hārith, the Lame, the greatest king of the Ghassānids, was held in considerable awe by the Byzantine Emperor Justinus.

Kinda was first mentioned in history about the fourth century AD. The founder of the Kindite dynasty, Hujr, was a stepbrother to the king of Himyar, who appointed him as ruler of the tribes of central Arabia. The Kindite kings soon spread their influence over the greater part of central and northern Arabia, becoming powerful rivals to the kingdoms of Hīra and Ghassān.

The story of Queen Zabbā and King Jadhīma

The first of the Lakhmid kings was Mālik. He was succeeded by his son Jadhīma Al-Abrash, a proud warrior prince whose turbulent and adventurous life became the subject of many legends and proverbs. Also famous in legend was his devoted wazīr, Qasīr, a wise and excellent statesman, a man of great cunning and shrewdness and a loyal friend to his lord.

It was the custom of the Arab kings to choose drinking or cup companions to provide entertainment in the form of story-telling, poetry recitals and witty conversations. Jadhīma, however, was so arrogant that he would have only the two brightest stars of Ursa Minor (Al-Farqadān) as his companions, believing no-one else was fit to sit with him. Whenever he drank wine, his servants filled two extra glasses which Jadhīma offered to the two stars, his heavenly cup companions.

One day Jadhīma heard that there was a very witty and handsome young man in the household of one of his relatives. He asked the youth to come to his court and become his page. Jadhīma had a sister and she soon fell in love with the king's new page and wanted to marry him. She summoned the page, whose name was 'Adi to her and revealed her feelings for him. Then she said, 'Use all your wit and charm to get the king

and his courtiers drunk. When he no longer knows what he is doing, ask him for my hand, making sure that the courtiers are witnessing his consent, for he is bound to agree.'

'Adi did as the princess suggested and, sure enough, the king agreed to the marriage in a moment of complete intoxication. The page went to his wife that night. In the morning the king saw him come out of the princess's room. 'What are you doing here?' bellowed the angry king.

'I have just left my bride's chamber,' answered 'Adi, trembling.

'Unlucky man, what bride are you talking about?' demanded the king.

'Your sister, my king. You agreed to our marriage only last night,' stammered 'Adi.

When the king realized what had happened, he flew into a terrible rage, vowing vengeance on his sister for daring to wed a lowly page. The princess, however, rebuked her brother.

'It was you who gave me to this man in marriage. I knew nothing about it until my maids came with perfume and jewels to dress and prepare me. It is all your fault for drinking so much and for indulging in such wild merry-making.'

Jadhīma ordered his sister to be confined to her rooms and did not allow her to see anyone until she had given birth to a baby. 'Adi had suddenly and mysteriously disappeared and, with no-one else in the world to love, the princess lavished all her affection on her baby son whom she named 'Amr. When the child reached boyhood, the princess dressed him in his best clothes and jewels, perfumed him with the richest incense of Arabia and sent him to his uncle. Jadhīma took to the boy at once and decided to bring him up himself as his son and heir.

One day, as the boy was playing near the palace, he suddenly disappeared. A company of jinn had spotted him and, coveting him for themselves, spirited him away. Jadhīma searched for his nephew for many months without success, finally giving up in despair.

Some time later, in the early hours of a spring morning, two young men named Mālik and Aqīl, who were on their way to see the king, stopped to build a fire and cook their breakfast. A wild young man suddenly appeared in front of them. He was starving and his body was covered with dirt and bruises. He lay on the ground exhausted and begged their servant for food. The two men looked at him suspiciously.

'If you reject me, you will not reject my descent and my house. I am 'Amr, the nephew of King Jadhīma,' he struggled to say.

The two men knelt by the young man and helped him to his feet. They made him comfortable, bathing and dressing him in their own best clothes, then they cut his nails and hair, which had grown long and wild. Finally they took him to the king. Jadhīma was so overjoyed to see the boy returned home safely that he promised to grant the two men anything they wished for.

'We have one favour to ask,' they said to the king. 'Make us both your cup companions for the rest of our lives.'

The king readily agreed and so it was that Mālik and Aqīl gained an honour that had previously been granted only to the stars.

In the fertile lands of northern Mesopotamia

and eastern Syria there ruled a king, who was also called 'Amr bin (the son of) Zarīb. 'Amr and Jadhīma were deadly rivals for the control of the region and were always fighting.

King 'Amr bin Zarīb had two daughters, Zabbā and Zabība. Zabbā, the elder, was a warrior princess of great courage and such dazzling beauty that poets compared her to the goddess Al-Zuhara. She had long flowing hair that reached to her ankles and streamed behind her when she went hunting or to war on her noble white mare. Both sisters were known for their commonsense and shrewdness.

King 'Amr decided to attack Jadhīma in one final attempt to defeat him. Unfortunately Jadhīma's armies were too much for him and he was killed in battle. Zabbā was chosen by her people to succeed her father and to celebrate her accession to the throne, she built two impregnable fortresses, one on either side of the River Euphrates, one for herself and one for her sister. Between them ran a secret underground passage dug as a precaution against a surprise attack.

Not for one moment did Zabbā forget the most sacred and binding of all Arabian customs: her father's death must be avenged by the shedding of his enemy's blood. Day and night she listened to the king's spirit clamouring for revenge as it flew helplessly and forlornly about the world, thirsting for the blood of the man who had killed him.

At length, the queen decided she had waited long enough. She told her advisors and leaders of her intention to march against Jadhīma. While she was speaking, her sister, Zabība, was weighing the matter up carefully. 'If you go to war against Jadhīma, you may either lose or win,' she said to her sister. 'In either case, you cannot avoid war breaking out again. However, you yourself may be killed, and then not only will your life be lost but your kingdom will go to Jadhīma as well.'

'You have spoken well, my sister,' replied Zabbā thoughtfully. 'I had not considered it like that. War will not solve our feud.'

So the queen decided to resort to trickery and deceit. She wrote to Jadhīma telling him she was not strong enough to rule alone as queen and

that she found the burden of government too much for a maiden to bear alone. 'Among all Arab kings and princes,' she added, 'you alone are my equal in birth and rank, you are the man most worthy of me. Our kingdoms would enjoy lasting peace and greater prosperity if they were united. Come to my court and I will be your queen.'

Jadhīma was surprised by the queen's letter at first but he was flattered and his pride and arrogance soon overcame his suspicions. 'She is a helpless young girl,' he thought to himself and decided to take up her offer and to travel to Zabbā's country to celebrate the marriage. When he told his court of his decision, Qasīr, his wise councillor, advised him strongly against the proposed marriage. He implored Jadhīma not to take the queen's words at their face value but to investigate her motives further before making a visit to her kingdom.

The king, deaf to Qasīr's warnings took no notice. He left for Zabbā's land from a place called Baqqa, riding in a great company of courtiers, and servants, followed by a long train of camels loaded with gifts for his future bride. After a while Qasīr again begged the king to change his mind. Again Jadhīma refused to listen.

'The matter was settled at Baqqa,' he said, using words which passed into a proverb.

However, as he and his retinue approached Zabbā's capital, Jadhīma was alarmed to see that her troops and cavalry seemed to be everywhere he looked.

'What do you suggest we do?' he asked Qasīr.

'You left all advice in Baqqa,' replied Qasīr, again using a phrase which was to become a proverb.

The queen's guards came out to meet the king and welcomed him as they would any monarch. Jadhīma was perplexed.

'Now what do you make of this, Qasīr?' he asked.

'Danger masking as ceremony,' replied Qasīr. 'If the queen's cavalry ride in front of you, the woman is genuine and I am wrong but if they surround you and ride behind you, then she is a traitor. My advice to you is to get on your swift mare, Al-'Asa, and to ride for your life.'

Yet again Jadhīma took no notice; he was a
proud man and a king; he did not want to run
away like a coward. Before he had time to give it
more thought, however, Zabbā's troops had
surrounded him, taking him back to the palace
more like a prisoner than a future king. But
Qasīr was too fast for them; he sprang onto the
back of Al-'Asa, the swiftest of all Arab horses,
and was gone like the wind.

Zabbā received Jadhīma at the foot of her
throne. She looked down at him disdainfully,
enjoying his humiliation. Something about her
dark, menacing beauty made his blood run cold.
Her flimsy clinging dress and the cruel glow in
her enormous eyes made her look like a goddess,
a vengeful goddess like Al-'Uzza, who was
always thirsty for the blood of victims. 'So, do
you see your promised bride, Jadhīma?' she said
to him in a dangerously soft tone.
'I see that I have reached my end,' Jadhīma
replied. 'My soil has dried up and treachery is
staring me in the face.'

Zabbā smiled triumphantly and turned to her
maidens. They took Jadhīma and laid him on the
floor. Then they placed a bowl beneath his
hands and cut the veins in his wrists, while
Zabbā watched in cold satisfaction. She poured
out some wine and passed a glass to Jadhīma,
who drank defiantly from it.

Before the king had arrived at her palace, a
fortune-teller had warned Zabbā not to let one
drop of Jadhīma's blood fall outside the bowl, or
his death would be swiftly avenged. So now she
was especially careful, warning her women, 'Be
careful not to waste a single drop of his blood,
for the blood of kings cures madness.'

Jadhīma was overcome with faintness and
soon his hands fell to the ground. A few drops
of blood fell outside the bowl.

'Don't waste the king's blood,' Zabbā called to
her servants in alarm.
'Mind not the blood so foolishly wasted by its
owner,' cried the dying Jadhīma. Like the earlier
words, his sentence became a proverb.

Meanwhile Qasīr had ridden without stopping
until his horse, Al-'Asa, had dropped dead with
exhaustion. Sad at heart, Qasīr hurried back to
Hīra on foot, where he told the king's nephew,
'Amr, the bad news. 'It is your sacred duty to
avenge your uncle,' Qasīr told him.
'I could never get anywhere near Zabbā,' he
objected. 'She is as unassailable as the eagles in
the air.'
'Leave that to me,' said Qasīr mysteriously, 'but
you must promise me your support.'

Then Qasīr did something very strange. He
cut off his nose and ears, then ordered his men
to whip him. His people could only think that a
hidden plan lay behind his actions. 'Surely some
great purpose has driven Qasīr to cut off his
nose,' they whispered to one another.

In her impregnable castle Zabbā was filled
with foreboding. She summoned the fortune-
teller to the court and asked her anxiously, 'Tell
me, reverend mother, what will happen now?'
'Amr's schemes will bring about your death but
you will not die at his hand,' prophesied the old
woman. 'You yourself will end your life.'

Zabbā was determined to avoid her fate. She
commanded one of her people, an artist, to go to
Hīra and try to join 'Amr's court.
'Use all your charms to tempt them with your
art,' she instructed him. 'When they come to
trust and accept you, I want you to paint 'Amr's
likeness in every posture that you can: sitting
and standing, mounting his horse and resting,
eating and sleeping. Then hurry back here. I
must know every detail of this man who plots

my death; I must know his face as I know my own.'

Meanwhile Qasīr had perfected his plans in Hīra and now rode to Zabbā's country pretending to seek her help. When she saw his mutilated face and terrible wounds, she asked who had been responsible. Qasīr told her it was 'Amr, who blamed him for Jadhīma's death. 'I have left his court for ever,' Qasīr told her. 'Let me serve you, O queen and you will be the greatest queen in the world.'

Zabbā hesitated. Qasīr was well known for his cunning and his loyalty to Jadhīma, and for some time she remained uncertain whether to accept or refuse his offer of service. But Qasīr, intent on his purpose, persisted in his attempts to gain her favour, taking every opportunity to prove his devotion and his skills as an indispensible statesman. Against her better judgement and the warning of her sister, Zabbā began to trust and rely on him. She did not forget the threat of 'Amr, however. When the artist returned from Hīra she often spent long hours gazing at the pictures he had made of her enemy so that his face haunted her by day and by night. And as a last protection, she wore on her finger a ring impregnated with a deadly poison.

One day Qasīr said to the queen, 'You ought to have a secret passage dug for you, so that you would have a means of escape if you were trapped.' Zabbā revealed to him that she already had one and showed him the tunnel under the Euphrates.

Sometime later Qasīr asked the queen if he could return to Hīra to collect his possessions and money and to trade for her on the way. He promised to bring back the goods for which Hīra was famous, robes woven with gold, silk, incense and perfumes. Qasīr travelled to and fro many times, on each occasion returning with priceless goods, for this was all part of the plot that he had devised with 'Amr. On his last journey from Hīra, Qasīr's caravans were not laden with rare silk and perfume, but with men concealed in sacks, led by 'Amr himself.

From her tower, the queen watched the weary camels with their heavy burdens walk slowly through the city gates. She shuddered slightly as she felt more than saw something unusual about the pace of the camels. But Qasīr did not give her enough time to think. As the last camel came through the gates, 'Amr and his men leaped out of their sacks and killed every man in Zabbā's garrison. The queen ran for her secret passage only to find Qasīr waiting there for her with his sword drawn. She swung round to see a man blocking her way, cutting off her retreat. She froze, gazing at him in horror, for his was the face that had haunted her dreams for so long. 'No! Not one of these men will boast of having killed me,' she said to herself, 'I am the warrior queen, Zabbā, the daughter of 'Amr bin Zarīb, whom none could kill in battle. I will be mistress of my own destiny right to the end.' So Zabbā lifted her hand to her mouth and sucked the poison from her ring. Before the two men could reach her, she fell dying.
'By my own hand, not by 'Amr's . . .' she whispered defiantly, with her last breath using words which, as a proverb, are still used today.

The year of the elephant

The last of the independent Himyarite kings was defeated by an army from Abyssinia about the middle of the sixth century. Their commander, Aryāt, was killed by one of his own men, Abraha, who was later appointed viceroy of Yemen by the king of Abyssinia.

Abraha had heard a great deal about the Sacred House of Mecca, the devotion it inspired and the deep respect in which it was held by the Arabs. He also noticed that the pilgrimage to Mecca seemed to be turning from a purely religious affair into a commercial and political event, reflecting the growing feelings of nationalism among the Arabs.

The new viceroy toyed with the idea of taking Mecca by force in order to destroy its religious influence and take control of its growing trade, but rejected this in favour of a diplomatic approach. He built a magnificent high temple in Yemen's capital, San'a, and called it Al-Qalīs; with this he hoped to attract pilgrims away from Mecca.

'The temple is so beautiful, it must have some useful influence over them,' he thought.

Before long, however, the temple was desecrated by a man from one of the tribes of Mecca who suspected Abraha's true motives. Furious at what had happened, Abraha now swore to reduce the Sacred House of Mecca to ruins, in revenge.

Abraha prepared for war, then set off for Mecca at the head of a great army, preceded by a long column of trained elephants, each carrying a number of skilled warriors. The first attempt to oppose him, led by a young Yemenite chieftain and his tribesmen, was crushed ruthlessly. Tribe after tribe surrendered to him as he advanced because no-one had the power or the numbers to match him.

When Abraha reached Tihāma, near Mecca, he ordered his army to seize all the herds of camels and sheep that belonged to the chieftains of Mecca. Among them were two hundred camels, the property of Abd Al-Muttalib, who was lord of the tribe of Quraysh, custodian of the sacred Ka'ba and later to become the grandfather of the Prophet Muhammad.

Abraha sent a messenger to Abd Al-Muttalib. He found the custodian praying in the Sacred House and read Abraha's message to him: 'I have not come to conquer you but to destroy your temple,' read the messenger. 'If you do not oppose me I will spare your lives.'
'We have no wish to fight your master, for we are no match for him,' replied the lord of the tribe of Quraysh.

The messenger then invited Abd Al-Muttalib to come to Abraha's camp. The Prophet's grandfather was a tall man of striking appearance and with an imposing presence. When he entered Abraha's pavilion, Abraha's councillors whispered to him, 'This is the lord of Quraysh who feeds the poor of the plains and the beasts of the wilderness.'

Abraha was so impressed with his guest that he descended from his throne and sat with him on the carpet, welcoming him warmly.
'What do you want from us, lord of Quraysh?'
'I wish you to return the two hundred camels that your men took from me,' Abd Al-Muttalib replied simply.

'When I first saw you I admired you,' replied Abraha, 'but now I talk to you I find you lacking in both dignity and common sense. You are aware that I have come to destroy the Sacred House of your forefathers and yet you sit here and discuss the fate of a mere two hundred camels!'

Abd Al-Muttalib, serene and dignified, showed no sign of confusion. He spoke calmly, 'I am the lord of the camels. I defend what belongs to me. The Sacred House has a far mightier lord who will surely guard it against all evil.'
'But he shall not succeed against me,' exclaimed Abraha.
'That is for you to say, not for me. I merely request the return of my camels,' replied Abd Al-Muttalib quietly.

Still puzzled, Abraha ordered the camels to be restored to the lord of the Quraysh and Abd Al-Muttalib returned to his people. Not long afterwards a delegation representing the tribes of Mecca and their neighbours asked Abraha if he would accept a third of their possessions and wealth in exchange for the safety of the Sacred House—but Abraha refused scornfully. Seeing that violence was inevitable, Abd Al-Muttalib told his people to take refuge in the mountains and they fled in terror and despair, leaving only their lord behind to pray in the Ka'ba. Abd Al-Muttalib took the ring of the door in his hands and cried, tears streaming down his face, 'Let thy will be done, O God. You have the strength to help or hinder their plans against you. Let it be as you wish.'

As the first golden rays of the morning sun touched the hills and sand dunes around Mecca, the invading army advanced towards the empty city. Abraha smiled to himself in triumph. What could stop him now? Mecca lay deserted before him. Suddenly his elephant, the noblest of his herd, the strongest and the largest, halted in his tracks and stood motionless. Nothing could move him; he seemed turned to stone. When Abraha's men tried to goad him with sticks, he knelt down and refused to get up. But when they turned his head the other way, towards Yemen, he stood up eagerly and began to walk back in that direction as though suddenly

released from an overwhelming restraining force.

As the elephant headed steadily away from Mecca, the sky darkened with the shapes of thousands of strange green birds flying from the sea, each carrying three stones in its beak and claws. The birds formed themselves into a vast army in the sky and swept over Abraha and his terrified men, flying low and dropping the stones as they passed over. The stones contained a deadly poison and whoever was hit died instantly of a terrible plague. Abraha himself was struck and died in agony beside hundreds of his men, who lay sprawled out on the sands like dried sheaves of corn.

The people of Mecca began to return cautiously to their homes. A lonely young widow, who had been a bride only a few months ago, walked with the jubilant crowd of women and children. As she walked, she felt her unborn child move inside her, impatient to be born.
'Your grandchild will be born soon, lord of Quraysh,' whispered the mother of the child who was destined to be born Muhammad, the Prophet of God.

Priests, soothsayers and wise men

The pagan Arabs firmly believed that priests had familiar spirits who were either jinns or demons. This personal contact with the supernatural gave them knowledge of both past and future and ensured the priests a privileged position in ancient Arabia; they inspired both awe and fear in people's minds. When a jinnee spoke through his mouthpiece, the priest, the message was delivered in a special kind of rhymed prose *(saj')* which added to the mystery.

The jinns who served the priests went to great trouble to satisfy their masters; they were known to eavesdrop on the angels by forming a ladder of bodies right up to the very edge of heaven. As the angels talked in their heavenly mansions the jinnee at the top of the ladder listened and passed the information to the one below and so down from jinnee to jinnee to the priests.

Some priests assumed additional roles: they acted also as orators, physicians, wise men and judges. It was not uncommon to find the chief of the tribe combining the functions of the priesthood, leadership and arbitrator. Many women of noble birth or special powers, like Zarqā Al-Yamāma with her gift of long sight, were also known as priestesses and witches and were held in great awe by their tribes.

The pagan Arabs were a superstitious people, who set great store by good and bad omens. Besides priests, therefore, there were many soothsayers, clairvoyants and diviners, who also played an important part in ancient Arabia. Most of them used everyday objects as sources of information: they gazed into bowls of water and mirrors; examined the hearts, bowels and livers of animals; drew auguries from birds and animals and cast pebbles or grains of wheat to interpret their patterns.

For some of the soothsayers, who depended mainly on careful observation, the arts of divination and the interpretation of omens developed into a highly specialized science called *firāsa*. This they divided into two forms: physiognomy, the art of judging character from a man's face, and the gift of second sight.

One of the most respected skills in ancient Arabia was the art of tracking, of which there were also two kinds: the tracking of footprints and the tracing of a man's family history by observation of his character, gestures and likeness to others in the group or tribe.

The dream of the King of Yemen

One night, after a day of celebration and festivity in honour of a recent victory, a king of Yemen had a very disturbing dream. When he woke up in the morning he found that he could not remember any of the details of his dream but its troubling influence remained with him throughout the day. It bothered him so much that he cancelled all his scheduled audiences and called his priests and soothsayers to ask them if they could remind him of his dream, so that the details would come back to him. No-one could help him. He looked so disconsolate that his mother, who was a priestess herself, suggested that he should speak to the other priestesses. 'For the oracles and jinn who serve the priestesses are cleverer and more sensitive than those that wait on priests,' she said to him.

The king summoned all the priestesses but, as before, none could help him. Feeling frustrated and annoyed, he set off to hunt with just a few of his servants. After a while, he realized that, while he had been lost in thought, he had strayed away from his men. He began to be worried, especially as the noonday sun was making him feel sick and faint. Suddenly he spotted a few dwellings at the foot of the hill some distance away. He spurred on his horse and headed for the furthest and most isolated. As he approached, an old woman came up to him and smiled in welcome. 'Dismount in peace, for you are quite safe with us. There is plenty of food and fresh water to restore your strength.'

The king made his way into the woman's simple home and sat down. It was very cool and a gentle breeze, which seemed to come from nowhere, soothed and calmed his thoughts until he drifted into a deep sleep. When he woke up a young woman of incredible beauty was standing beside him. She smiled at him and said, 'May no shame blemish your name, O king. Would your majesty care to have something to eat?'

The king gave her a suspicious look. How could she know that he was a king?

The girl noticed and tried to reassure him.

'Great lord, king born of kings, you have done us a great honour by coming here today. Do not let mistrust cloud such a special occasion.'

The girl then brought the king food and drink and entertained him graciously until he began to relax in her company. He watched her in fascination, feeling himself drawn more and more to this unknown girl.
'What is your name, fair maid? he asked her gently.
''Ufayrā, my lord,' she replied.
'How did you come to address me as king?' he enquired.
'Because I know you are the king whom neither the priests nor the jinn have been able to help remember a forgotten dream,' said the girl.
'Do you know what my dream was?' the king asked anxiously.
'Yes, my lord, it was no ordinary dream.'
'That is so, but can you tell me what I saw?'
'Ufayrā's eyes clouded and she appeared to gaze at images she alone could see.
'You saw storm follow storm, in a tumult of glowing clouds and swirling light. You saw a rushing river and you heard a clear voice calling, urging you to drink. You watched those who drank flourish and those who refused wither and perish.'

The king was astonished.
'That was indeed the dream I had,' he said, 'but what ever does it mean?'
'The storms are crowned kings and the rushing river is knowledge and wisdom. The voice that called the people to the river belongs to a prophet to come. Those who drank will follow him, those who abstained will oppose him.'
'What will this prophet who will inherit our throne call for? What will he ask of us?' asked the king, still amazed by the girl's knowledge of his dream.
'He will ask us to fast and pray and to be kind to kith and kin,' replied the girl. 'He will ask us to get rid of all our idols and to turn away from the path of sin.'

The king gazed at the strange girl with thoughtful, dreamy eyes. Her beauty and her wisdom fascinated him and he could think of nothing else. Before he was able to put his feelings into words, however, she forestalled him by saying, 'My oracle is both loyal and jealous. To love me brings woe and to desire me only causes sorrow.'

Regretfully the king bade her farewell and returned to his palace. There he commanded his men to drive a hundred camels across the desert to 'Ufayrā's house as a gift to the priestess who had read his dream and set his mind at rest.

Satīh predicts the fall of the Persian empire

The legendary figures of Shiqq and Satīh stand out among the priests and seers whose extraordinary powers of clairvoyance were celebrated in many tales and poems.

Shiqq and Satīh were born on the same day and lived to an extremely old age. Shiqq was half a man: he had only one eye, one arm and one leg. Satīh was boneless except for his skull; his people used to fold him like a robe to carry him from one place to another. His face grew in his chest as he had no neck or head. Kings consulted both of these strange men about their dreams. The following story tells how the Persian emperor sent his messenger to Satīh to interpret the dream of his grand wazīr.

On the night of the Prophet Muhammad's birth, fourteen of the battlements on the great hall of the Chosroes (the *Iwān*) in Persia collapsed into heaps of broken stone. The Persian emperor was filled with foreboding, for he believed that the damage to the hall of kings was an evil omen. The next morning, at his daily meeting with his advisors and emissaries, he listened in horror to reports of other strange events: sacred fires which had burned for centuries in the temples had gone out for no reason; lakes had dried up overnight and rivers stopped in their courses. Then, to make matters even worse, the emperor's grand wazīr came up to him, his face pale with anxiety and lack of sleep, and said, 'I have had a dreadful dream, my emperor. I saw countless Arabian stallions and camels cross the River Tigris in triumph and spread everywhere over our land.'

'Do you know of anyone, who can interpret the

70

significance of what befell the great *Īwān* and also explain your own dream?' the emperor asked.

'I do not know of anyone,' replied the grand wazīr, 'but the governor of Hīra, if asked, would I am sure, send you one of his wise men.'

The wise man came from Hīra, but when he was told of the emperor's problem had to admit that his knowledge was not adequate to unravel the mystery of the fourteen fallen battlements and the grand wazīr's dream.

'But,' he continued, 'I have an uncle in Syria whose name is Satīh. He is the greatest oracle alive. If it pleases your majesty to send me to him, I will bring him to you.'

The emperor sent an escort with the wise man and they set out for Syria. They travelled without stopping until they reached the place where Satīh lived in solitude. However, when they entered the small, bare cell, they found Satīh lying on his bed apparently dying. His nephew tried to restore him but in vain. Then he tried shaking him.

'Listen to me, Satīh, the great emperor, the lord of the Persians, who fears neither the thunder of heaven nor the rumblings of fate, has sent me to you as his messenger,' he said to his uncle.

At last Satīh raised his head and opened his eyes. Gasping for breath, he whispered, 'On the backs of camels you came to find Satīh dying; now the gap between him and his grave is rapidly narrowing.' He continued with a tremendous effort, chanting slowly, 'The lord of the sons of Sasān sent you because of what happened to his *Īwān*, because his fires were extinguished and his wazīr anguished. He saw camels and horses cross his rivers and pursue his forces. Tell your king that when the message of God is delivered, Syria will no longer be Syria and Persia no longer Persia. Fourteen kings and queens shall rule in the hall just as fourteen battlements of the *Īwān* were seen to fall, before fate reveals what it has in store.'

The messenger and his escort returned at once to the emperor who sighed with relief when he heard Satīh's prophecies.

'It will be many years before the last of fourteen kings is born, brought up and crowned,' he said, 'there is plenty of time.'

What the emperor did not realize was that the fourteen kings were destined to rule for only forty years, at the end of which time, Satīh's words were all to come true. Amid the clatter of horses hooves, the lowing of camels and the sounds of marching feet, wave after wave of Muslim soldiers crossed the desert to attack the Persian empire and change the political map of the world beyond all recognition.

The four clever brothers and the lost camel

An Arabian chieftain died leaving everything he had to his four sons. He was a wise man and knew that his sons might quarrel about their inheritance. Before he died he told them that if things should go wrong between them, they should consult his friend, another chieftain, and the king of Najrān who was known for his sound judgement. Sure enough, the brothers could not agree about how to divide their inheritance and after quarrelling for a long time, decided to follow his instructions.

The four brothers set off to visit the man they had chosen to settle the dispute between them. On the way they noticed the tracks of a grazing animal. The first brother said, 'The camel that was grazing here was blind in one eye.'

The second brother looked closely and said, 'it is lame in one foot.'

'The tail is missing,' said the third.

'It must have strayed from its owner,' concluded the fourth brother.

After a while, they met a cameldriver running in their direction. He shouted to them, 'Have you seen a stray camel?'

'Was it blind in one eye?' asked the first brother.

'Was it lame?' asked the second.

'Was it without a tail? asked the third.

'Yes, do you know where it is now?' asked the cameldriver eagerly.

'We haven't actually seen it, but if you go back the way we came, you might well find it,' answered the fourth brother. So the man left them to continue searching for his camel.

Later that evening, he met the brothers again

in the market place in the city of Najrān where they were resting.

'I did not find my camel,' he told them.

'Did your camel carry a load of corn on one side?' asked the first brother.

'Did it carry a load of honey on the other side?' asked the second brother.

'Was it being ridden by a pregnant woman?' asked the third.

'Yes,' answered the cameldriver in reply to all three questions. 'Did you see anybody take it?'

'We have never set eyes on your camel,' the fourth brother told him.

The cameldriver was now quite convinced that the four brothers had stolen his camel. He followed them until he saw them going into the king's palace. Before the guards could stop him, he had rushed into the king's presence.

'O king, these four men stole my camel and hid it away,' he exclaimed. 'They have described my camel to me in the greatest detail yet they deny having taken it.'

The king turned to the four brothers and asked them what they had to say in their defence.

'On our way to this city we saw the footprints of a camel by the road,' said the first brother. 'I noticed that it had eaten the grass on one side of the road only, so I guessed that it must have been blind in one eye.'

'I saw that one of the tracks was less distinct than the other, so it must have been lame,' said the second brother.

'I noticed that the camel's droppings were all in one heap, so I realized that it must have been without a tail, or its droppings would have been scattered,' said the third brother.

'The camel had grazed in many places,' said the fourth brother, 'yet while it had missed some of the spots where the grass was thickest yet it had lingered where it was scarce. Therefore I inferred that it must have gone astray.'

The cameldriver was not fully convinced.

'But how did they know it was loaded with corn and honey and that it was carrying a pregnant woman?' he argued.

'Ants and flies were swarming over something in the road in several places,' replied the first brother. 'When we looked more closely we noticed that it was honey and corn.'

'We found some human hairs where somebody had obviously dismounted to rest,' said the second brother. 'They were so long that they must have belonged to a woman.'

'We observed handprints where the woman had sat down by the roadside,' said the fourth brother. 'From the use of the hands we guessed she must have been heavily pregnant.'

The king turned to the cameldriver.

'These men have spoken the truth,' he said. 'They merely observed your camel's tracks; they did not steal your camel.' The king turned next to the young men, asking them their names and tribes. When he discovered who they were, he asked his steward to take them to his guesthouse and make them comfortable. To one of his bright young pages he gave a whispered message, asking him to follow the men and to listen carefully to everything they said.

The steward brought the guests some fresh honey.

'We have never tasted sweeter and fresher honey than this,' they said.

'That would be true, brothers' said the first

brother, 'but for the fact that this honey was collected from the skull of a dead giant.'

At dinnertime the steward grilled a lamb which the brothers ate with great appreciation. 'We have never tasted such tender and juicy meat,' they said.

'That would be true, brother' said the second brother, 'but for the fact that this lamb was fed on a bitch's milk.'

After dinner the steward brought them some wine to drink.

'We have never drunk such clear, pleasant wine,' they said.

'That would be true, brother' said the third brother, 'but for the fact that this wine came from a vine that grew on a grave.'

The brothers told the steward, 'We have never been entertained more generously. The king's hospitality is beyond compare.'

'That would be true, brothers,' said the fourth brother, 'but for the fact that this king is not the son of his father.'

The page, who was listening to them, returned to report to his master. The king was very disturbed by what the page told him and went at once to find his mother.

'In the name of God,' he said to her, 'tell me who my father was and who I am.'

'What a strange question,' hedged his mother. 'You are the son of your father, the dead king, of course.'

But the king persisted until in the end his

mother confessed. 'My son, your father the king, whose name you bear, was an old man when we were married. I feared that if we did not have a son and heir, the crown would go to another house. A young prince came to visit us, so I offered myself to him and became pregnant.'

Then the king summoned the steward and asked him about the honey, the meat and the wine.

'I was told that a swarm of wild bees was seen not far from here,' said the steward, 'so I asked my men to go to collect their honey. When they reached the spot they found that the bees had built their hive inside a huge skull. In spite of that the honey was of a rare quality so I offered it to your guests. As for the lamb, my lord, the shepherd who sent it said that it was a yearling and the best in the herd. Its mother died just after it was born but it so happened that the shepherd's bitch produced her first litter at the same time. The lamb was lonely until it joined the young puppies feeding from their mother. The wine came from a vine that grows by your father's grave, a vine whose fruit is unmatched for quality and abundance throughout the land. The king marvelled at the brothers' powers of observation and intuition. He entertained them royally for several days; then he settled the dispute between them, showered them with gifts and saw them off on their way back home.

Proverbs and fables

Proverbs form an important part of the literary heritage of ancient Arabia. It was thought that the author of many of these sayings was a wise man called Lukmān. According to tradition, God offered Lukmān the choice of being either a prophet or a wise man and he chose to be a wise man. He was, however, a man of many roles, known as a holy man, as a wazīr or councillor, a judge and an arbitrator who helped to keep peace among the tribes.

Arab and Muslim storytellers added to the legends surrounding Lukmān until he came to represent all the Lukmāns mentioned in the myths. In particular he became merged with Lukmān, the son of 'Ād, whose adventures with the seven falcons symbolized man's eternal struggle against time and fate.

These are just a few of the many proverbs of Lukmān:

Perhaps a brother may be given to you, though not born to your mother.

He who does good has good done unto him.

Walk quietly, lower your voice, for the voice of the ass is the loudest and most ugly of voices.

'Which of your deeds is most worthy of you?' Lukmān was once asked. 'Abandoning that which does not concern me,' was his reply.

Lukmān was also famous for his fables—short anecdotes which made a moral or philosophical point in story form. Some of the fables are very similar to the famous Greek fables of Aesop and Lukmān is often called the Aesop of the Arabs. These fables here are typical examples.

The sick stag A stag once fell ill. His many friends came to visit him, and ate all the herbs and grasses which grew near his cave. When the stag recovered, he went in search of something to eat, but he found nothing. He died of hunger.

The woman and her hen A woman once owned a hen which laid a silver egg every morning. The woman thought, 'If I give her more food, she will surely lay more eggs.' She doubled the amount of food but the hen, unable to take it, died of overfeeding.

The Wind and the sun The sun and the wind argued between themselves as to who would succeed in stripping a man of his clothes. The wind roared and raged, bellowing with its utmost violence, so the man, feeling the cold, gathered his clothes about himself more tightly and the wind could not remove them. Then the sun rose and shone fiercely. As the day grew older the heat increased gradually until the sands and rocks burned with it, so the man of his own free will took off his clothes, gathered them in a bundle and went on his way.

The Mosquito and the bull A mosquito once alighted on the horn of a bull. Thinking that she must be a heavy burden to him she said, 'If I have caused you any inconvenience, I promise I shall fly away in a minute.' The bull answered mildly, 'I did not notice you when you alighted, and I shall not feel you when you fly off!'

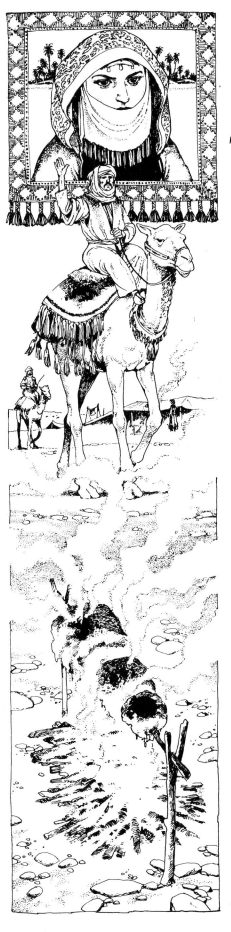

Tales of generosity, honour and loyalty

The tribal structure was the nucleus of social and political life in ancient Arabia. Each tribe was divided into clans and each clan comprised a group of families. The individual owed undivided and absolute loyalty to his clan first and to his tribe second. The bond of clanship was expressed by the term *'asabiyya*. It was based primarily on blood ties but membership of a clan was not absolutely a matter of birth. Strangers, freed slaves who wished to remain near their former masters and people seeking refuge, were all admitted and fully absorbed into clans and tribes. The sharing of food, or the sucking of a few drops of blood, were sufficient to create a powerful bond of brotherhood and kinship comparable to blood relationship. Often, because of the threat from rival tribes, a number of weak or smaller tribes would swear loyalty to one another and thus form a confederacy. *'Asabiyya*, therefore, frequently broke the bounds of clan and tribe and was applied to a larger concept based on political and social factors rather than on the primitive concept of mere blood kinship.

As the spirit of the clan was expressed in the term *'asabiyya*, so the virtues most revered among the desert Arabs were embodied in the word *murū'a*. *Murū'a* represented the unwritten code of honour, of manly excellence, chivalry and gallantry, held and recognized by all the tribes of the desert. *Murū'a* policed the desert more effectively than any authoritarian legal system. It was a private, rather than public code, demanding total commitment from the individual, even when he was alone or far away from his tribe. Later, the tribe would usually celebrate any good deed in poetry dedicated to the occasion.

The concept of honour was an important aspect of *murū'a*; to preserve his personal honour, or the honour of his tribe, the pagan Arab would willingly sacrifice his life. No tribal lord could hope to survive if he lacked the attributes of honour: he must be free of blame and shame, courageous, hospitable, chivalrous and proud. *Murū'a* also implied patience in the face of hardships, bravery in war, forbearance and the protection of the weak; the giving of refuge to all who sought it, whatever the consequences; the opposition to injustice and perseverance in seeking blood revenge. The code demanded of the ancient Arabian that he faced victory, defeat and death calmly and with fortitude; that he answered calls for help with speed and always kept his word; that he was faithful and loyal; guarded well anything entrusted to him for safekeeping; and most of all *murū'a* demanded that he was always generous.

Hospitality and kindness to guests and strangers are often essential for survival in the desert but these were not just regarded as virtues. They were elevated to mythical proportions by the poets of the desert. Figures like *Hātim of Tayyi'*, for example, known as the most generous of Arabs, became legends, famous for a heroism far more refined in spirit than the heroism of the battlefield.

Self-sacrifice and unquestioning devotion were essential for friendships which not even death could dissolve. But the ancient Arab was also a deadly enemy; he never forgave an injury or refrained from avenging it.

These qualities of nobility and heroism were not the monopoly of men. There were many Arabian women whose sense of honour, eloquence and courage, generosity of spirit, passionate loyalty and gracious manners were celebrated in verse and legend.

The ideals of the pagan Arabs lived on, given a new dimension and impetus by Islam which regarded them as essential components of the true believer's character and spiritual life.

Hātim of Tayyi'

Hātim was the son of a lady of noble birth called Ghunayya. Ghunayya was known even while she was a young girl living with her brothers for her generosity and kindness, especially to wayfarers and travellers. As she grew up, her brothers decided to withhold all her money from her as she gave everything she had away. One day, as a test of her will-power, they gave her a score of camels with a strong warning not to give them away. It was not long before a woman from a neighbouring tribe, who came to see her every year, begged her for something to ease her poverty. Ghunayya immediately gave her the camels saying, 'I have been hungry myself, so I would never say no to anyone who seeks my help.'

Some years later, after Ghunayya had married Hātim's father, she had a strange dream. She heard a voice asking, 'Which would you prefer—to give birth to a boy whose name will be Hātim and who will be generous of deed and spirit or to give birth to ten boys all as brave as lions and fearless on the battlefield?'
'I choose Hātim,' she replied without hesitation.

While still a boy, Hātim used to take his share of food and walk with it to the road. There he

would invite passers-by to sit down and eat his food with him. If the road was empty and there was no sign of any travellers, he would leave his food untouched by the side of the road and return. His father noticed Hātim's behaviour and decided that his son needed something more to occupy him. He gave him a herd of camels to look after, a mare and a slave girl. Instead of taking the camels to graze, however, Hātim drove them to the road and waited. Some riders approached him. 'Have you anything for us to eat, boy?' they asked.

'How can you ask when you see all these camels?' Hātim replied. Then he chose three of the finest camels and killed them for his guests. 'We only wanted you to give us some milk to drink,' said the men, surprised by the boy's generosity.

'I am aware of that,' said Hātim, 'but I guessed from your clothes that you are from far away and I wanted to give you something to remember me by and to talk about when you go home.'

It so happened that the three men were famous poets and they were so impressed by Hātim's generosity that they each made up a poem in his praise. Then it was Hātim's turn to be overcome.

'I wished to be hospitable to you but your kindness has made my deed seem small by comparison. I swear by God to kill every camel in my herd unless you accept them as a gift to divide between you.' He looked so determined and serious that the men felt compelled to accept. Each took ninety-nine camels and they went on their way.

Hātim returned home empty-handed, his face glowing with pride.

'Where are my camels?' asked his father.

'O father, don't grieve for your camels. Instead of them I have brought your house everlasting fame and glory. I traded the camels for songs and poems that will live for ever.'

'You did that with my camels?' his father roared.

'I did,' replied Hātim calmly.

'You and I will never share the same roof again as long as I live,' said his father. That very day the father packed up his possessions and left, taking the rest of his family with him and leaving Hātim alone with his slave and his mare.

As Hātim grew to manhood, so his legend grew with him. His fame, both as a poet and as a generous host, spread far and wide across the desert. His poems and the poems composed about him were recited by the campfire at night to men and children who gazed spellbound trying to see through the darkness the figure of the knight-poet whose bounty the very sands of the desert had known, and whose hospitality and care for the weak and the poor made the cruellest of man tremble with pity and admiration. Perhaps one of the most popular stories about Hātim was that of his marriage to Māwiyya, the daughter of 'Afzar, whom she succeeded as queen.

Māwiyya was a proud and self-willed woman who used to marry and divorce whoever she wanted among the handsome men of her people. One day she asked her servants to look for the most attractive man in Hīra. They searched everywhere until by chance they came upon Hātim. Here is the man we want, they thought, and took him to their mistress.

Māwiyya found him attractive and invited him to her bedroom. He refused because he said that he was waiting to find out about two friends whom he had lost earlier. She offered him food and wine, but again he declined. He had vowed, he said, not to eat or drink until his friends had eaten and drunk first. When the queen promised to send her men to look for his friends, he insisted on going with them. The queen eventually allowed him to go and the missing men were found at last. Instead of returning to Hīra, however, Hātim persuaded them to escape.

'If we stay here,' he told them, 'we will become the queen's slaves and to me death is preferable to dishonour.'

When Hātim was safely back at home he found it difficult to forget the beautiful and wilful Māwiyya so he decided to return after all to Hīra and ask her to marry him. When he reached her court, however, he discovered she already had company. Two other men had come to ask for her hand in marriage: one of them was the famous poet, Al-Nābigha. Māwiyya asked each of them to go away and compose poems celebrating their courage and generosity.

'I shall marry the most generous and poetic amongst you,' she declared.

As soon as the three suitors returned to their camps, each killed a camel and prepared to eat. Unknown to any of them, Māwiyya had disguised herself as an ordinary woman and now she approached each suitor in turn, asking them for food. The first gave her a very poor piece of meat; the second gave her the camel's tail but Hātim made her wait while he prepared the best meat from the most tender part of the camel.

That evening, each suitor sent a camel-load of presents to the queen but Hātim also sent similar presents to all the women in the neighbourhood. The next morning Māwiyya asked her suitors to recite the poems they had written. When it was Hātim's turn, she listened especially carefully. Afterwards the queen invited the three men to a meal at which she ordered her serving maids to offer each suitor exactly what he had offered her the night before. But Hātim refused to eat until the other two suitors, who now bent their heads in embarrassment, agreed to share his food. 'Hātim is the most generous and the most eloquent man among you; therefore I am going to marry him,' said Māwiyya to her guests.

However, Māwiyya's life with Hātim was far from easy because he never kept anything for himself or his family. Whatever he owned or came by he divided among the needy or gave to those who sought his hospitality or help. Once, a year of severe drought came which caused the earth to split into cracks and furrows. There was little food or water and mothers' milk everywhere dried up so that the crying of the young could be heard in the stillness of the night. Hātim and his wife sat up one night with their three children until the early hours of the morning, trying to soothe their hunger with promises. At last they fell asleep but, as the stars were fading, the corner of Hātim's tent was lifted and a woman's voice called, 'I am your neighbour, Hātim. My boys are wailing like hungry wolves. Please help me for I don't know what to do.'

Hātim went out to her and said, 'Bring the boys here. God has provided for you and them.'

The woman left only to return in a few minutes with two babies and four small children, barely able to walk with hunger. Hātim went to look for his beloved mare. She neighed contentedly when she saw Hātim, who looked at her sadly and patted her gently. Then he drew his knife and killed her, tears clouding his eyes. He skinned and quartered her; then he made a fire and fed the starving family on grilled meat. Calling all his neighbours, he distributed what was left among them. They too, built more fires and sat eating while Hātim, wrapped in his cloak against the cold of the morning and the piercing pangs of hunger, squatted on the sand and watched happily. He refused to share in the meat in case someone went hungry because of him.

Another time Hātim was travelling far away when he met a prisoner being led by his captors. The prisoner recognized him and begged him to set him free by paying his ransom.
'It is not fitting that you ask me for help when I am empty-handed, alone and far from my people, but I will do my best,' replied Hātim.

Hātim arranged with the captors that they would accept a sum of money in exchange for the prisoner's freedom. Then he persuaded them to take him prisoner instead.
'My wife will pay the ransom I promised once she learns that I have been captured, so you have no need to keep your prisoner,' he said to them. They agreed reluctantly. Hātim sent messengers to his wife asking her to pay his ransom and, when she did so, he too was set free.

After Hātim's death, his son 'Adi and his daughter, Safāna, followed in their father's footsteps, feeding those in need, entertaining travellers and giving refuge to all who sought the protection of their father's grave. But Hātim's spirit could find no rest or peace; it roamed the desert looking for the lonely and hungry, always alert to the sound of approaching footsteps.

One story has it that some riders set up camp not far from Hātim's grave. One of the men climbed on to the grave and shouted, 'Entertain us now if you can , Hātim.'

His companions warned him to be careful. 'How can you slander a dead man who did you no harm?' they said, rebuking him.
'His tribe keeps boasting that nobody has ever sought Hātim and not been entertained by him. Let me see Hātim entertain us now!' he mocked.

That night the man who had jumped on

Hātim's grave woke up and called for his camel.
'What is the matter?' his friends asked.
'While I was asleep Hātim came to me and killed
my camel so that he could offer us hospitality,'
said the man.

The camel was indeed dead. The three men
built a fire, cooked the camel and ate.
'Hātim has entertained us even though he is
dead,' they said to each other.

The next morning, as they were riding away, a
man leading a black camel stopped them.
'I am 'Adi, the son of Hātim. My father came to
me while I slept and told me he had killed one of
your camels to entertain you. He ordered me to
give you this black camel in return.'

The men accepted the camel and went on their
way, marvelling at what had taken place.

Giving refuge

Fukayha was a woman of noble birth. One day
her tribe planned to ambush an outlaw who had
recently raided their camp. The outlaw, whose
name was Sulayk, was well known as a fast
runner so Fukayha's tribesmen lay in wait for
him by the spring. When he grew thirsty and
had drunk deeply, he would not be able to run
so fast, they reasoned. Their plan succeeded and
Sulayk was on the point of being captured when
he rushed into the nearest tent, which happened
to belong to Fukayha, and asked her for refuge.
As the men of her tribe ran in after him, she
threw her cloak over him, drew a sword and
stood between him and the men. When she
realized they were determined to capture
Sulayk, Fukayha did something no free woman
would do unless she was desperate: she tore off
her veil, uncovered her hair and cried for help.
Her brothers came at once to her tent.
'I have given refuge to this man, I beg of you to
defend him for me,' she said to them.

The brothers drew their swords, swearing to
kill any man who dared to lay hands on the man
to whom their sister had given refuge. The
tribesmen withdrew reluctantly; the outlaw's life
was saved and he escaped into the desert
unharmed.

Forgiveness

There was once a man called Qays, the son of 'Āsim, whose wisdom and forgiving nature were proverbial among the Arabs.

One day, while Qays was talking to a group of friends, some men from his clan came up to him carrying the body of his dead son and pushing his nephew, whose hands were tied behind his back, in front of them.
'This man killed your son. Decide what you want to do with him,' they said.

Qays appeared not to show any agitation or loss of control and continued to talk to his guests. When they had left, he turned to his elder son.
'Go to your cousin, my son, and set him free. Bury your brother and then go to comfort your mother, for she is a stranger to this land. Take a hundred camels to her as a gift; perhaps that will ease the pain a little.'

Self-sacrifice

There was a man called Ka'b who was once travelling home with his people during the hottest month of the summer. One day they were stopped by a stranger who asked if he might join them. The travellers agreed and they continued on their journey through the desert.

It was not long before they lost their way and discovered that their water was running out. There was no spring in sight and the only way to survive was to ration what little water was left between them. Each man was allowed a small cupful which they stopped to drink once a day at nightfall. One evening, when it was Ka'b's turn to drink, he noticed that the stranger was staring at him. He immediately turned to the water-bearer and said to him, 'Give the water to our brother, the stranger.' So the stranger drank Ka'b's share of the water.

The next day the same thing happened again. The stranger drank and Ka'b went without. In the morning when it was time to leave, the people called to Ka'b to stand up and mount his camel.

'Get up Ka'b. We are not very far from water now. Soon you will be able to drink.'

But Ka'b could neither move nor answer. Sadly, they covered him with his cloak to protect him from the desert vultures and left him. So Ka'b died that the stranger might live.

Loyalty

Imru l-Qays was one of the greatest poets of the ancient Arab world. He was the son of the ruler of Kinda but a usurper killed his father and deprived Imru l-Qays of his inheritance. One day he decided to go to Constantinople to seek the help of Justinian, the Byzantine emperor, hoping to avenge his father's death and win back his kingdom. Before he left he collected together all the family armour—weapons, coats of mail and shields—and gave them to a fellow poet named Samaw'al, the lord of a neighbouring country, to guard for him while he was away.

Justinian received the Wandering King, as he became known, and agreed to help him by giving him an army. Imru l-Qays then set out for home and he was almost there when he was overtaken by one of the emperor's messengers. The messenger gave him a valuable present, a

richly woven cloak. As soon as Imru l-Qays put it on his shoulders, ulcers appeared all over his body and he died a slow and painful death. It was believed that the emperor plotted to kill Imru l-Qays because he and the emperor's daughter had fallen in love.

When the usurper of Kinda heard of Imru l-Qays's death, he travelled to Samaw'al's country to claim the possessions that the wandering king had left in Samaw'al's care. He marched on Samaw'al's fortress with a great company of soldiers and laid seige to it. Samaw'al and his family managed to shut themselves safely inside the fortress but his son, who had been out hunting when the army attacked, was captured by the enemy as he tried to return home. The soldiers bound the young man with strong chains and placed him just under the walls of the fortress, where he could easily be seen. Then the king called out to Samaw'al.

'What do you wish to say to me?' asked Samaw'al, looking down from the battlements.

'Your son is my prisoner. If you hand the arms that have been entrusted to your safekeeping over to me, then he will go free. If you refuse, I will kill him before your very eyes,' replied the king of Kinda.

Samaw'al did not hesitate. His proud answer reached his enemy loudly and clearly: 'I shall not break my pledge or betray my trust,' he replied. 'Do as you wish.'

Then the king drew his sword and killed Samaw'al's son with one thrust in front of his anguished father. The soldiers kept up the siege for only a few more days before they withdrew. Samaw'al watched them ride away empty-handed until the last man had disappeared in the distance, then said these lines slowly to himself: 'I have kept my word to the dead king and have guarded his weapons. Let others break their promises, I shall always be true.'

Honour

Mundhir, the king of Hīra, had two favourite cup companions. One night, he became very drunk and grew so angry with his friends that he ordered his servants to bury them alive. The next morning he could remember nothing of what had taken place and went to look for his friends. When he learned what he had done to them, he was overcome with remorse and grief. To keep the memory of his friends alive he had two obelisks built by their graves, which were known as *Al-Ghariyyān*, meaning blood-stained. For two days every year he sat by the graves to

do penance: the first day he called the Day of Good Deeds because whoever first came to him on that day was given a hundred black camels; the second he called the Day of Evil Deeds for whoever met him first on that day was offered in sacrifice to his dead friends and his blood was poured over their graves.

Every year Mundhir kept up the custom of the two days of penance. One day a man from Tayyi' called Hanzala, came to visit the king. 'May no shame blemish your name. I have come to you as a guest,' said Hanzala.

'Alas, I have to offer you as a sacrifice, for today is the Day of Evil Deeds,' replied the king sadly.

'But I am your guest, O king,' cried the shocked Hanzala. 'You have always been hospitable and generous to both me and my people.'

'I have no choice,' said the king, 'but before you die you may ask me one favour.'

'Grant me one year of grace so that I may settle my affairs and provide for my family,' Hanzala begged. 'I promise to return after one year.'

The king agreed but on one condition. 'Provide me with a guarantee of your return and you may go.'

Hanzala looked around the king's courtiers.

He recognized the face of a worthy and honourable man called Sharīk whom he asked to act as his guarantor. Sharīk immediately agreed. 'May no shame blemish your name, O king. I offer my hand for his hand, my blood for his blood, should he not return at the appointed time,' he said to the king.

The year passed and the day came for Hanzala's return. There was no sign of him and Sharīk went to the king to offer himself in his place. Already the woman appointed to mourn for him had begun to lament his impending death. The swords-man prepared to execute him and was on the point of raising his sword, when far away in the distance a rider appeared galloping towards them. As he drew near everyone was very surprised to see that the man was Hanzala of Tayyi', returning to keep his word. He was already wearing his burial shroud and was accompanied by his mourning woman.

The king was so moved by the loyalty of the two men that he set them both free and rewarded them for their honourable conduct. He then declared that the barbarous custom of sacrifice on the Day of Evil Deeds was to be abolished and forgotten.

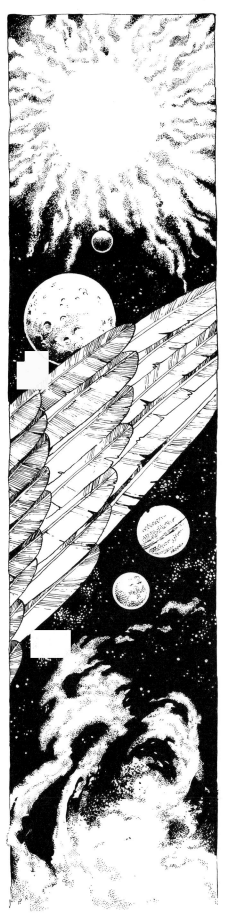

Celestial and terrestrial worlds

The prophet Muhammad was born in Mecca in the Year of the Elephant, so called by Arab historians in memory of the failure of Abraha's campaign against Mecca and the Sacred House.

Muhammad's date of birth is fixed around AD 570. He started life as an orphan, for his father died before he was born and his mother died while he was still a child. The boy Muhammad was brought up by his grandfather Abd Al-Muttalib, the lord of the tribe of Quraysh and the custodian of the Sacred House. After his death Muhammad was cared for by his uncle Abu Tālib.

In AD 611 the first verses of the Koran were revealed to Muhammad when the Archangel Jibrīl appeared to him in a vision and commanded him in the name of God to preach His Word as His Messenger and Prophet to the nations of the world. The Koran is therefore, to Muslim believers, the Word of God revealed to Muhammad through the Archangel. The Sayings of the Prophet Muhammad *(Hadīth)* and his teachings, the Traditions *(Sunna)* are considered to be a kind of supplement to the Koran.

Islam means 'submission to God'. Like Judaism and Christianity before it, it called for the worship of the one God. This concept was not totally unfamiliar to the Arabs in the pre-Islamic times, for the Hanīfs, the descendants and followers of Ibrāhīm, had kept the tradition of the worship of a single God alive in Arabia before the coming of Islam.

By the end of the seventh century (the first Islamic century), the armies of the Muslim Arab caliphs, the successors of Prophet Muhammad, had dominated the whole of Arabia, overthrown the Persian Empire in Iraq and Iran, expelled the Byzantine Empire from Syria and Egypt and penetrated as far east as the Indus and Caucasus and as far west as the Atlantic.

The new world of the Muslim Arabs was a world rich with the heritage of the ancient cultures and religions of the Near East. The Arab genius, newly awakened and full of vigour, absorbed these older cultures, blending, unifying and forging them into a dynamic new civilization.

This chapter and the ones that follow are mainly concerned with the myths and legends of the Muslim Arabs. As Islam continued to spread and encounter other civilizations, Arab popular imagination gave rise to new myths and tales reflecting the diversity, the complexity and the richness of the new world. Most striking amongst them are the myths and legends woven about the creation of the universe as an ordered whole comprising the celestial world (of the skies) and the terrestrial world (of our earth).

It is important to distinguish between the Koranic account of the creation and the myths later constructed about it, so it is helpful to start with a brief summary of the Koran's version.

In the Koran, God created the earth, the mountains and everything in the world in four days.

'He set upon the earth mountains towering high above it. He pronounced His blessing upon it and . . . provided it with sustenance for all alike. Then He made His way to the sky which was but a cloud of vapours, and to it and to the earth He said: "Will you obey me willingly, or shall I compel you?" "Willingly" they answered. In two days He formed the sky into seven heavens and to each He assigned its task.'

Then God covered the lowest of the heavens with bright guardian stars, made the sun and the moon and fixed their courses. Next He created the angels and the jinn. Then he planned to create Ādam to be His viceroy on earth. When the angels knew of their Lord's intention, they objected, lest Ādam should defile the new world with the shedding of blood. But God replied, 'I know what you do not know.' After He had created Ādam, God taught him the names of everything in the world and then He summoned the angels and asked them if they could name everything He had created in the world. The angels did not know so God ordered Ādam to name them. Then the Lord said to the angels, 'Did I not tell you that I knew the secrets of heaven and earth?' He ordered all the angels to prostrate themselves before Ādam. All bowed to him except Iblīs.

The Sayings of the Prophet, the Hadīth, add more details to this account, mainly providing explanations of the nature and order of creation. Contributions came also from the Muslim sages and mystics (Sūfīs) and from the interpreters of the Koran and the Hadīth.

Folklore and popular religious literature, however, produced many highly coloured versions of the story of creation and the workings of the universe, myths influenced by ancient Arabian and ancient Mesopotamian sources and further enriched by Greek, Persian, Indian and Judo-Christian thought. It is these colourful myths that provide the accounts in this chapter.

The order of creation

Accounts differ as to the order of the creation. One version states that first God created the waters and then placed His divine Throne upon them. Then He caused vapour to rise from the water. It rose and spread over the water so God called it the sky. Next God caused the waters to thicken and harden till they became earth, which He then made into seven earths. But the earth needed a support so God placed it on the back of a whale, whom He called Nūn. He made the whale live in the water upon a rock. The rock was borne upon the shoulders of an angel, whose feet rested on another huge rock borne by the wind. But since the whale could not keep still and caused the earth to tremble, God created the mountains to support it. Then He made His way up to the sky and moulded it into seven heavens.

In another account the first thing to be created was the sacred Pen with which everything that happened from the day of creation to the day of judgement was recorded; this, it was said, was created even before the waters for in the beginning there was nothing but air above, and below thin cloud.

The most colourful of the accounts concentrates on the creation of the earth. When God caused the foam and the water to harden, the first part that became earth was the sacred grounds of Mecca, then He laid the rest of the world around it. Next He divided the earth into seven layers and commanded an angel to carry them. The angel left his place below the Lord's Throne and flew downwards until he was right underneath the lowest layer. Then he spread his arms to the east and to the west and carried the

The celestial world

The traditional Islamic view of the universe divides the celestial world into seven heavens. One religious account, however, gives this description of the seven heavens. Each heaven is separated from the other by five hundred years' walk.

The first heaven, which is made of steam and vapour has the colour of burnished iron; it surrounds the earth of mankind like a giant dome in which God has hung the planets and the stars. The angels who live here are made of fire and wind and are under the command of the angel Thunder, who looks after the cloud and rain. While they work the angels chant: 'Praise be to Him whose is the kingship and the kingdom.'

The second heaven is made of iron and the angels who live there are multi-coloured. Their chant is: 'Praise to Him, the Lord most Mighty.'

The third heaven is made of copper and is inhabited by angels with either one, two or four pairs of wings. Each angel has a different voice and face but none is said to recognize the others, so intent are they on their daily prayers. Their chant is: 'Praise be to the everlasting, the eternal Lord.'

The fourth heaven is made of white silver. The angels there never stop praying whether they are standing or kneeling. All the time they chant: 'Holy and most high is our Lord, the Compassionate. There is no God but He.'

The fifth heaven is made of gold. The angels who live here will never lift their heads from their prayers until the day of judgement when they will say: 'O Lord we never worshipped you as we should have done.'

The sixth heaven is made of green sapphire. There live the Karūbiyyūn, a race of angels of the highest order who serve as the mighty army of God. They stand around the Throne and act as God's messengers to the people of earth.

The last of the heavens is the seventh heaven, the home of the supreme angels, the greatest except for the bearers of the Throne and the Spirit (al-Rūh).

Each angel of the seventh heaven is unique. The might of their wings defies description; for

layers of the earth on his shoulders. But the angel had nothing to stand on, so God sent him a bull with forty thousand legs and seventy thousand horns. When the angel placed his feet upon the bull's back they trembled and the earth shook. The Lord took a rock of green hyacinth, measuring five hundred years' travel in length, and placed it between the bull's back and his horns, to steady the angel's feet. It was believed that the bull's horns protruded from under the earth, and since it had its face under water, its breathing caused the sea to ebb and flow. Now although the angel could stand firmly, the bull had nothing to support it. God therefore made a great green rock, as thick as the seven earths and seven heavens put together, and placed it under its hooves. Then He ordered the whale, Nūn, to carry the rock which was borne upon the wind, which, in its turn, rested upon the divine power.

when they are poised to fly, even the smallest feather is enough to enfold totally our earthly world. The colours of their wings are like a kaleidoscope, shedding an ever-changing, dazzling light. They stand in rows, chanting with their eyes lifted to the divine Throne, never ceasing to contemplate it.

Beyond the seventh heaven there is nothing but an enormous, glowing cloud, greater in size than the seven earths and the seven heavens put together, above which towers the Throne of God.

The Pen and the Guarded Tablet. The divine Throne of God and the Footstool, the Pen and the Guarded Tablet, the Tree of Salvation and the Celestial Sacred House all feature in the Koran or the Hadith. As with the story of creation and the universe, longer descriptions coloured by imagination are found in popular religious literature and it is from these that the following are mainly taken.

It was thought that God first created the Pen (*Al-Qalam*). Then He commanded it to write. 'What shall I write, O Lord?' asked the Pen trembling in awe.

'Write in the name of your Lord, the Compassionate, the Merciful. Write down the destiny of the world,' was God's answer.

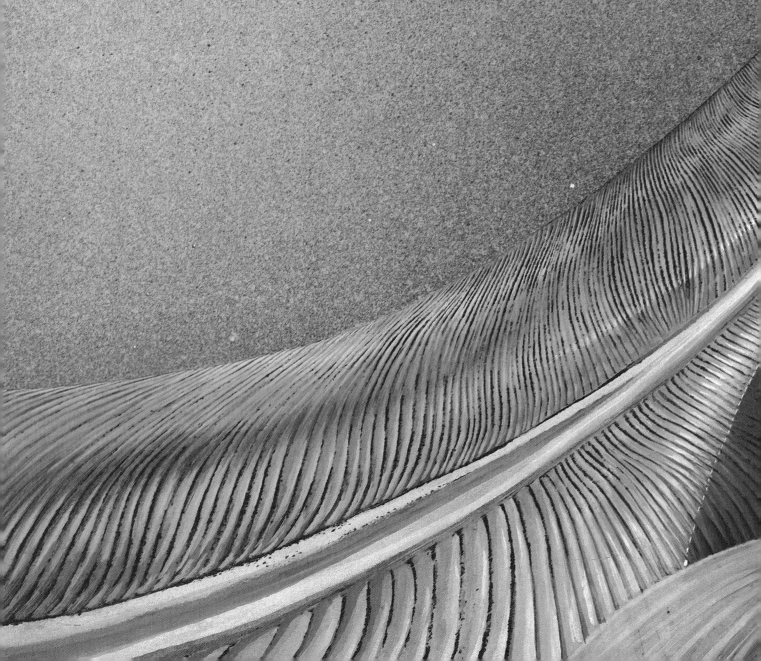

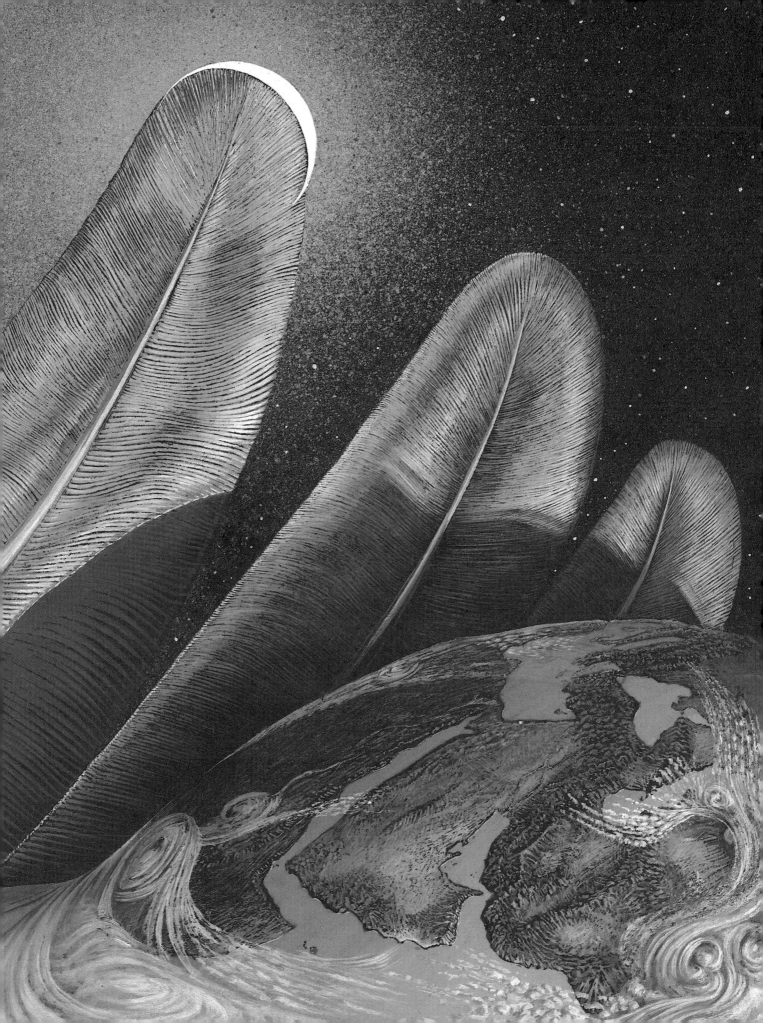

So the Pen moved by the will of God and faithfully recorded on the Guarded Tablet everything that happened from the day it was made until the day of judgement.

One account has it that the Pen, which was made of light, measured the span between heaven and earth, while the Guarded Tablet (*lawh Mahfūz*) on which the Pen wrote the destiny of mankind, measured the distance between east and west in width and the same span in length as the Pen. The Tablet was made of pearl with pages of brilliant ruby and the edges were encrusted with sapphire; it was held in place on the angel's lap who inscribed on it in light the words flowing forth from the Throne. Another account gives the responsibility for the Tablet to the angel Isrāfīl of the Trumpet of Resurrection, who is said to carry it hanging on his brow.

The Throne and the Footstool. The Throne of God (*'Arsh*) fired the imagination of all Muslims on both a popular and mystical level. The yearning to picture it in all its unearthly majesty and divine splendour led to some of the most evocative descriptions in Arab folklore and religious literature. It was created, according to most accounts, from a single red sapphire. In length and width it stretches over fifty thousand years' walk: in height it towers over the world like an enormous dome. A more mystical version views the Throne as a sphere, known as the Ninth Sphere, the prime mover of the rest of the spheres: the sun, the moon, the five planets and the fixed stars. Because no planet occupied its centre it was also called the Supreme Sphere and the Dark Sphere or the Sphere of Spheres.

According to another account the Throne was made out of a single brilliant pearl. It has four pillars for legs, each placed at a thousand year's flight distance from the other. It is decorated every day in seventy thousand cloths woven of light, so bright that no creature can look upon them and live. Beside the size of the Throne, the world appears like a small ring cast out into the wilderness. One story was told of an angel with eighteen thousand wings who was commanded by God to fly up to His Throne. The angel flew for twenty thousand years only to find he was barely touching the foot of one of the supporting pillars. So the Lord doubled the number of the angel's wings and increased his strength and asked him to fly up to Him once more. The angel flew for another thirty-thousand years but still he had only climbed as far as the top of that same pillar.

The Footstool (*Kursiy*) was believed to be at the foot of the Throne. It was shaped from one pearl of a size beyond description, encompassing both heaven and earth. It was thought to occupy the Eighth Sphere, the sphere of the fixed stars.

The Tree of Salvation. The Tree of Salvation, or the Tree of the Ultimate (*sidrat Al-Muntaha*) embodies the symbols of absolute bliss and peace, and the grace and light of God. Opinions differ as to where the Tree of Salvation, also believed to be the Tree of Paradise, stands. Some thought that it spanned the distance between the highest and lowest of the seven heavens; others that the blessed Tree stood in the middle of paradise, its branches spreading beneath the Throne. Two rivers, the Nile and the Euphrates, were said to issue at the foot of the Tree and flow out into our world and two other rivers, unseen to the world, issue and flow into paradise. The Tree's branches rise towards the ultimate, bathed in the many-coloured light of God, with innumerable angels flying around it like brilliant golden butterflies.

The Celestial Sacred House. The Celestial Sacred House, which served as the model for the *Ka'ba*, the Sacred House of Mecca, was placed by God in the seventh heaven. There, it was said, the Sacred House stands, lit by the ever-shining light of countless diamond lamps and eternal burners glowing with sapphire, pearl and emerald.

Within the seventh heaven, it was told, there is a sea of light into which the Archangel Jibrīl plunges once every day. When he emerges he shakes the shimmering light off his wings: seventy thousand drops fall from his feathers and from each an angel is born. As soon as the newborn angels are assembled they are commanded to praise the Lord in the Sacred House. Each day they are replaced by another seventy thousand angels as Jibrīl plunges into the sea of light and rises to shed light.

The sun and the moon. It was told that at first

God made the sun and the moon like two suns from the light of the Throne. However, it soon became apparent that the creatures of the world were unable to distinguish between night and day: they did not know when to wake or when to sleep, when to start working or when to stop because it was always daytime. So the Lord commanded the Archangel Jibrīl to dim the light of the moon by touching it with his wings.

The moon's light, once as bright as the sun's, became gentle, cool and silvery. The dark markings we see on its face are said to be traces left by the Archangel's wings.

Next God made a chariot from the light of the Throne to carry the sun on its course through heaven. The chariot had three hundred and sixty shafts and to each was assigned an angel in order to pull it. In the east and west God made one hundred and eighty setting places for the sun. The moon, too, had a chariot made from the light of the Footstool, with three hundred and sixty angels to help it on its course.

Beneath the vault of heaven God made a sea in which revolved the sun and moon chariots and the five planets, Mercury, Venus, Mars, Jupiter and Saturn. Unlike any other sea this one stretched like a tight-rope between east and west, with its waves suspended in space so that not one drop escaped from it.

The sun and the moon never emerge completely from the sea, for if they did the earth would be burned to ashes by the sun and the people of the earth would be so dazzled by the moon that they would worship it instead of God. The rest of the stars, it was said, are fixed to heaven, like lamps, revolving with the heavens, and praising God.

When the sun rises in its chariot in the east, the angel charioteers carry it across the sea of light to the west. If God decides to punish His creatures for their sins and remind them of His might, He commands the sun to fall out of its chariot into the sea to cause an eclipse. Then the angels pull the sun back into its chariot, allowing only a little of the sun's circumference to rise above the sea so that daylight can emerge after the darkness of the eclipse. They continue on their way to the setting place of the day in the west. There the angels hide the sun, as it falls below the horizon in our world.

In the far regions of the east and the west, the account continues, where the sun rises and sets, there live two races of people in two great cities with twenty thousand gates, each guarded by ten thousand men who are replaced daily. The noise their movements and voices make is said to muffle the sound of the rising and setting of the sun so that it can not be heard by human ears.

Once the sun has set, the angels from heaven

forward. 'I am the only one among you who can accomplish this task,' he said.

In spite of Emir Mūsa's objections the sheikh climbed the ladder, reciting verses of preservation from the Koran and calling on God for protection as he did so. But when he reached the top, he too began to clap his hands and wave at whatever it was he could see on the other side of the wall. The emir's men called up to him, begging him not to throw himself down like all the others. Slowly the sheikh sat down on the top of the wall and began to pray. The men below watched anxiously and after an hour he stood up and called down to them. 'Fear not for I have been saved from the devil by God.' 'What was it you saw in the city?' asked the emir.

'I saw ten beautiful maidens, as fair as the moon, beckoning me, tempting me to join them. Then I saw a lake at the foot of the walls that seemed to lure me down into its depths as it did our companions. As I started to pray so the vision began to fade and soon all I could see were fourteen dead men lying side by side,

outstretched beside the wall.'

The sheikh then walked cautiously along the top of the wall until he came to one of the towers of brass. He discovered that it had two gates of gold with neither padlocks nor handles to open them: in the middle of one of the gates was engraved a horseman of brass with a hand outstretched as if pointing. In the palm of the hand were these words: 'He who wishes to enter the City of Brass must turn the knob of my navel twelve times and the door will open for him.'

The sheikh turned the knob and sure enough, the gate opened with a great noise like thunder. Inside he found himself in a long passage that led down some steep steps to an enormous hall, the walls of which were covered in every imaginable kind of armour. There were shields, sharp swords, curved bows and long lances. Against the walls, on wooden benches, leaned row after row of dead men. At the end of the hall he came to another gate, securely bolted with chains and bars. The sheikh walked slowly back along the rows of the dead, wondering what he should do next. As he passed by, his attention was drawn to one of the dead men who must have been much older than the rest when he died. Hanging round his waist he saw what he had been looking for – a large bunch of keys. With these the sheikh opened the gate at the end of the hall and at long last the emir and all his men were able to enter the city.

All around lay the dead bodies of the guards, and gate-keepers, stretched on couches of silk. Wondering, they first decided to bury their dead friends beneath the city walls, then moved on to explore the strange place they had found. They came to a great market area which was lined on both sides with fine buildings and shops. The shop doors were open and inside they were well stocked with various goods and with copperware; but the merchants who sat inside as if still discussing prices were all dead, their bones dry and their skin shrivelled with age. On they went to the quarter where the silk merchants had lived, then to the jewellers' market, the shops of the money changers and the perfume merchants' bazaar. They marvelled at the heaps of brocade, of woven silks, of pearls, rubies, gold, silver, musk and amber they saw in the markets.

Yet one thing was always missing: they saw no trace of food among all the wealth and riches piled in the shops.

As they left the perfume market, they came to a magnificent palace decorated with lapis lazuli and gilded with great craftmanship. The emir reined in his horse and and sat contemplating the marvellous perfection of this palace. Its gate stood ajar and on it he read: 'Consider what you have seen, O man, and think carefully about the fate of those people who erected these graceful palaces. Of what use were their golden crowns and fair garments, their beauty and their charm, when destiny frowned at them and death fell upon them?'

The emir brooded silently for a while, then ordered his men to enter the palace. They walked down long corridors whose walls were covered with banners, unsheathed swords, golden shields and helmets. Then they came to an anti-chamber where, on ivory benches and seats encrusted with gold and covered with silk, lay stretched the figures of men whose skin had withered on their bones. Next they passed into a spacious hall containing four high pavilions decorated with gold and silver. In the middle of each pavilion stood a great fountain of alabaster under a canopy of brocade. The water from the fountains flowed into a pool with sides of many coloured marble. Inside the first pavilion were chests of red, yellow and white brocade and quantities of jewels, pearls, rubies, gold and silver. The second pavilion was full of finely wrought arms and armour; the third had chests containing weapons inlaid with gold and precious stones. In the fourth the chests were packed with eating and drinking vessels, plates of gold and silver, great platters of crystal, goblets encrusted with pearls and cups of cornelian. The men gathered as much of the treasure as they could carry and walked out of the pavilions, and the great hall, penetrating further and further into the palace.

As they reached the innermost rooms, they saw a great door made of teak wood inlaid with ivory and ebony and plated with shining gold. Over this hung a silk curtain, embroidered richly with emblems and patterns. This door,

too, was locked with a mysterious device and again it was the sheikh with his skill and knowledge who managed to open it. Beyond the teak door was a marble passage hung with tapestries showing birds and animals of red gold and white silver, their eyes made of pearls and rubies. At the end of the passage they came to a marble hall, its walls inlaid with precious stones. The polished floor appeared so slippery that the sheikh ordered it to be covered with blankets before he would cross it. In the middle of the hall they saw a domed pavilion made of stone but plated with red gold. The pavilion was crowned with a small alabaster dome decorated with tiny lattice windows fitted with bars of emerald. Under the dome they saw a canopy of brocade hanging from pillars of red gold, delicately patterned with figures of birds whose feet were made of green jasper. Below each bird hung a network woven with pearls; the nets joined in the middle to form a glowing veil under which stood a couch set with rubies, pearls and other precious stones.

On the couch lay a fair woman, as beautiful as the sun, whose loveliness surpassed any the emir and his men had ever seen before. She was dressed in a garment sewn with pearls. On her head she wore a crown of red gold over a head-band made of the rarest stones. On her forehead shone two great gems which glowed like two suns and round her neck hung a necklace of rubies and great pearls. On her breast was a jewelled amulet filled with musk and ambergris. She seemed to stare unflinchingly at two rare jewels which lay beside her, as if entranced by their beauty.

Emir Mūsa wondered at her delicate complexion, the rosiness of her cheeks and the raven blackness of her hair and, thinking, like all those who gazed at her, that she was still alive, he said, 'Peace be with you, fair maiden!'

The figure took no notice and the sheikh said to the emir, 'Know, emir, that she is dead and there is no life in her. What you see is a corpse that has been skilfully embalmed. The life that sparkles in her eyes is caused by quicksilver, cunningly placed in her eye sockets, beneath her eyeballs.'

'Glory be to God who conquers His creatures

by death,' exclaimed the emir. Then he approached the steps leading to the couch where the figure lay, but halted when he saw the statues of two slaves, made of copper and armed with swords as if ready to strike at any intruder. Between them the slaves were holding a golden tablet on which was engraved: 'Praise be to God the Creator, the Lord of lords, the Cause of causes, the Everlasting. O son of Ādam how ignorant and forgetful you are. Do you not know that death waits for you, preparing to seize your soul? Therefore make ready yourself to leave this world. Where is Ādam the father of mankind? Where are Nūh and his descendants? Where are the Caesars and the Chosroes? Where are the 'Amālikites and the giants of ancient times? All have perished, all reaped by God the Reaper.

'Know you who read these words that I am Tadmurah, the daughter of the kings of the 'Amālikites. I ruled fairly and justly over more lands than any king has ever possessed. Long did I enjoy happiness and ease till death and disaster knocked at my door. For seven successive years our city suffered the most terrible drought; no

rain fell and no crops grew. We ate all our stores and eventually had to slaughter all our cattle till nothing was left for us. Then I ordered my men to take all the gold and silver I had in my treasury and sent them out in search of food. After a long time they returned to us empty-handed and informed us that they had failed to trade the gold for food. There was nothing for us to do but to lock the gates of our city and resign ourselves to the will of God.

'We displayed all our wealth and valuables and sat waiting for death which presently fell upon my people so that they all perished.'

Emir Mūsa was filled with pity when he read these words but, almost blinded by tears, he continued to read: 'Indeed the fear of God is the greatest of virtues and death is the only certainty in this life. O son of Ādam, what has hardened your heart against your Lord and tempted you away from him? Where are the Kings of China and their mighty deeds? Where is 'Ād bin Shaddād and his soaring pinnacles? Where is Nimrod the wrathful? Where is Pharaoh, so cruel and sinful? Death has overtaken them all and the Almighty has spared no-one. Know you who come to this place that she whom you now see was not deceived by the world and its passing pleasures, and therefore she feared her Lord and made peace with Him. Whoever comes into our city and enters it by the will of God, let him take what treasures he wishes, only let him not touch or remove my clothes for these are the last traces of earthly modesty and wordly possessions left to me. Let him fear God and refrain from robbing me lest he bring down destruction on himself. Peace be with you and may God spare you!'

The emir stood for a while with tears in his eyes. Then he turned to his men and ordered them to fill their bags with as much treasure as they could carry. It was Tālib who protested. 'Surely we are not going to leave the queen's jewels and rich clothes behind? They would make the best present of all for the caliph.' 'Did you not listen to the queen's warning?' the emir asked, 'She has put her trust in us and we are no traitors, to betray her.' 'But she is dead and all this is nothing to her now,' replied Tālib. 'Let us just cover her with a cloth and remove her robes.'

Before anyone could dissuade him, Tālib had rushed up the steps towards the two slave statues. As he came between them, they moved suddenly, leaned forward and cut his head off with a mighty blow of their swords. 'You have brought this horrible death on yourself with your greed,' cried the emir, shocked at the sight. 'There was enough for all of us without taking what was not ours.'

With their camels loaded with treasure, the party prepared to depart. They closed the doors of the palace and locked the gates of the city behind them, then continued their journey along the coast, leaving the City of Brass and its silent inhabitants in peace.

Several days later they came to a high mountain and from its top, could make out black men, women and children dressed in hides, standing at the mouths of the caves which dotted the mountainside. The black people watched the strangers nervously, drawing together in fear. 'These are the people the caliph has sent us to search for,' said the sheikh so the emir asked his men to dismount and prepare to make a camp.

After a time, the black people realized they were not about to be attacked and their king came up to the emir and greeted him in Arabic.
'Are you humans or jinns?' he asked.
'We are humans but your own great size and this isolated place, where you live by the shores of an unknown sea, make me think that perhaps you are not,' replied the emir.
'O Prince, we are also, like you, the sons of Ādam. We are descendants of Hām the son of Nūh. As for this sea it is the sea of Karkar.'
'But how do you know about Ādam and our world, when no prophet could possibly have come to visit this remote corner of the earth?' asked the emir, surprised.
'A long time ago we worshipped our own gods,' said the king. 'Then one day a man came out of the sea, bathed in a strange light which spread out from him to the horizon. He said his name was Al-Khidr, the Green One, and called us to the worship of God and the love of Muhammad His Prophet. Still every Friday we see a light moving across the surface of the earth and a voice calling, "Holy is he, God of the angels and the Spirit. All blessings are in Him and there is no power but in Him."'

Emir Mūsa listened in wonder, then said, 'We are the subjects of the King of Islam, Abd Al-Malik and he has sent us here to solve the mystery of the copper vessels belonging to King Sulaymān. The caliph has commanded us to take back some of these and the jinns that are believed to be imprisoned inside them.'

The king agreed to help at once and ordered his divers to find some of the strange jars from the sea. He entertained the visitors for three days while the divers collected twelve jars which they handed to the emir. He in turn thanked his hosts with many presents. Then the emir and his men set off on the long perilous journey home. When at last they arrived back, the caliph received them eagerly and listened in fascination to the story of their adventures. Then the caliph opened the copper vessels. Out came the thick black smoke, gradually forming itself into the shapes of the imprisoned jinns. As the caliph and his people stood silently watching, the strange forms cried out loudly, 'We repent, we repent,' then disappeared for ever.

Journeys to the world of the supernatural

The Arabian Nights contains many stories in which the hero, after a short or long journey, slips without warning from the natural into the supernatural world. Sometimes the supernatural world seems to run parallel to the natural one, but all of a sudden a point of contact is established and they come together. The story of the Queen of the Serpents, which was written in the eleventh century or perhaps earlier, is a clear example of this kind of tale. In the original version, the main story provides a frame for two other separate tales, one of which is given here.

Once upon a time, there lived a very wise and learned man who enjoyed the love and respect of his people and his students. His one sorrow in life was that he had no son to follow in his footsteps and inherit his learning. One night, feeling sad and hopeless, the wise man prayed to God to grant him and his wife a male child to bring joy to their lives. Not long afterwards, in answer to his prayers, his wife became pregnant but before her term was completed the wise man had to go away on a journey. As he was returning, his ship was wrecked in a storm and all his valuable books were lost except for five pages which he managed to rescue.

When the wise man reached his home at last, he said to his wife, 'I feel the hour of my death approaching and I shall soon leave this world of change for the eternal one. If you give birth to a boy after my death, call him Hāsib and bring him up well. When he is old enough to ask for his inheritance from me, give him these five pages. If he understands their contents, he will become the wisest man of his time.'

Then the wise man said farewell to his wife and closed his eyes for ever. Only a few days after his death his wife gave birth to a baby boy whom she called Hāsib. The astrologers who drew the baby's horoscope told her that Hāsib would have an unlucky start in life but that if he survived the early years he would live long and happily. When Hāsib was five, his mother sent him to school but he did not learn anything there. Despairing of him, she took him out of school and apprenticed him to a craftsman, but again the boy failed to learn what he was taught. Some of the woman's neighbours were woodcutters and they advised her, 'Buy your son a donkey, a rope and an axe and send him with us to the mountain to cut wood. We shall divide the price of wood between us and that will enable him to support both you and himself.'

Hāsib's mother was overjoyed at the offer. She bought Hāsib the things the woodcutters had recommended and sent him off with them to work. All went well until one day a sudden heavy rainstorm forced the woodmen to seek shelter in a cave. Hāsib was feeling restless and he sat by himself in a corner, tapping idly on the floor with his axe. One place gave a hollow sound so he began to dig and soon uncovered a round flagstone with a ring in its centre. Hāsib called to the woodcutters and showed them what he had found. Together they managed to lift the flagstone and discovered a trapdoor underneath it. When they had opened the trapdoor they found a large vat full to the brim with honey.

Hāsib offered to sit by the vat and guard it while his comrades went to collect some jars and pots to carry the honey away. The vat was so large that it took the woodcutters several days to transfer the honey and sell it in the city and all the time Hāsib sat watching by the vat. Honey was a very valuable substance and the greedy woodcutters decided to get rid of Hāsib in case he tried to claim for himself the money they had made from selling the honey. When they returned to the cave for the last time, they told him he must go down into the vat to collect the last few drops of honey. No sooner was Hāsib inside, than they moved the trapdoor and then the flagstone back into place, leaving Hāsib there to die.

At first Hāsib shouted for help but even if his cries had been able to penetrate the cave floor, there was no-one there to hear him. After shedding helpless tears for a while, he started to explore his prison. He found the vat was in fact a deep well and on one of the walls he could just detect a faint light which seemed to come from a small hole. He took out his knife and began to enlarge it until it was big enough for him to creep through. Hāsib found himself in a long corridor at the end of which was a great door of black iron, fastened with a silver padlock and a golden key. He opened the door and walked for a long time until he came to a lake, in the middle of which he saw something shining brilliantly. He waded in and swam until he reached an island of green jasper, on which were twelve stools. In the centre was a beautiful throne so he climbed on to it and sat down to rest, thinking about his strange journey. Before long he fell fast asleep.

Hāsib was awakened with a start by a great noise of movement and a loud hissing sound. When he opened his eyes he was terrified to see that each of the twelve stools was occupied by a large serpent with eyes glowing like red coals. Hāsib trembled with fear, and slipped off the throne, trying to look as inconspicuous as possible. The serpents remained still.

After a while a serpent as big as a mule came up to him carrying on her back a great tray of gold on which lay another serpent. This one shone like crystal and had a beautiful human face. The shining serpent greeted Hāsib in a clear voice and was then placed on the throne. Presently all the other serpents slithered down from their stools and bowed to her. She turned to Hāsib. 'Have no fear of us, young man, for I am the Queen of the Serpents. I bid you welcome! But you must tell me who you are and where you come from.'

Still trembling, Hāsib ate the food he was offered and told how he had been betrayed by the woodcutters.
'Nothing but good will come to you from this,' said the Queen of the Serpents reassuringly, 'but you must stay with us for a while for now I am going to tell you my story and all the wonderful adventures that have happened to me.'

Hāsib settled down to hear what she had to say and the Queen of the Serpents started to tell her tale.

The adventures of Balūqya

There once lived in Cairo a wise and pious Jewish king who had a son called Balūqya. As he lay dying the king summoned his wazīrs and nobles and asked them to help his son to rule his country, and to look after the boy when he had

died. Balūqya succeeded his father and reigned wisely and justly, guided by his father's wise councillors until one day he discovered an ebony casket in his father's treasury. Inside was a silver casket and inside that was a book. Balūqya began to read and found that the book contained a description of the Prophet Muhammad and how he would be sent by God to mankind in the future as His chosen Prophet. The king was so filled with longing to meet this prophet that he summoned his advisors and told them that he was leaving his kingdom to wander in the world in the hope of meeting Muhammad.

After short preparations Balūqya said his farewells to his sad mother and set off for Syria. It was not long before he came to the sea and, finding a ship ready to sail, he eagerly went on board. One day the ship dropped anchor off an island and the king went ashore to explore. It was very hot and he sat down to rest, soon falling asleep. When he awoke he discovered to his dismay that the ship had sailed without him so he set off once more to explore the island. He was surprised to see that it was inhabited by serpents as big as camels and palm trees, who prayed and chanted, calling upon God to bless Muhammad.

'Who are you and what is your name? Where do you come from?' they asked Balūqya as soon as they saw him. So Balūqya introduced himself and told them his story.

'But who are you, O noble creatures?' asked Balūqya in turn.

The serpents told him they were some of the inhabitants of hell, created by God to punish the unbelievers.

'How do you come to be here?' Balūqya asked again.

'Know, Balūqya, that because of its tremendous boiling heat, hell breathes in and out twice a year. When it breathes out in the summer we are cast out of its belly, and when it breathes in, in the winter, it draws us back inside again. This happens to us because we are small compared to the full-grown serpents of hell.'

'How do you come to know about Muhammad?' asked Balūqya.

'His name is written on the gates of paradise, for God would not have created the world but for Muhammad. This is why we love him,' they replied.

Balūqya was deeply impressed by these words and even more convinced that he must continue his journey. He soon found a ship which took him to another island. There he landed and after walking for some time, met another group of serpents, both large and small. Among them was a white serpent whose body shone like crystal, lying on a golden tray carried by a great snake the size of an elephant.

'Now this serpent, O Hāsib, was none other than myself,' said the Queen of the Serpents. 'I greeted Balūqya and asked his name, his country and his business. He told me about himself and then asked who I was. "I am the Queen of the Serpents, Balūqya," I said, but seeing that he was impatient to continue his search, I sent him on his way asking him to greet Muhammad for me if he should meet him.'

Balūqya travelled on until he reached Jerusalem and there he met a man called 'Affān who was learned in all the sciences and in the art of magic. 'Affān was fascinated by the ancient stories of King Sulaymān. He had read in one book that after his death, Sulaymān was laid in a coffin which was then transported to a place beyond the Seven Seas where no ship could ever go. Sulaymān's magic ring was buried with him and now no human or jinnee could hope to remove it from his finger. In another of his books 'Affān had read that whoever wore Sulaymān's ring would have power over humans, jinns and animals. In yet another he had read about a herb that, if rubbed into the soles of the feet, enabled a man to walk on the surface of the sea without getting wet. This herb, the book said, could only be obtained with the help of the Queen of the Serpents.

'Affān was impressed by Balūqya's piety and invited him to stay in his house as his guest. He listened spellbound to the king's account of his adventures and to the purpose of his quest but was especially interested in Balūqya's chance meeting with the Queen of the Serpents.
'If you can arrange for me to meet the Queen of the Serpents, I can make it possible for you to meet the Prophet Muhammad when God sends him to mankind in time to come,' 'Affān said. 'If we manage to capture the Queen of the Serpents and carry her to a certain mountain, the herbs themselves will tell us their properties as we pass them by. But the Queen must be with us. There is a herb that will enable us to walk on the surface of the sea without wetting even the soles of our feet and with this we can cross the Seven Seas to Sulaymān's burial place and take the ring from his finger. Once we have the ring, we can wish for anything we like; we will be able to cross the terrible Sea of Darkness and drink from the waters of immortality which lie beyond. Then, if God wills, we will be able to wait for the coming of Muhammad.'

Bulūqya agreed to take 'Affān to the Queen of the Serpents so long as he promised not to harm her and they set sail for the island where she lived, taking an iron cage with them.
'There, Hāsib,' continued the Queen of the Serpents, 'they put two bowls of milk and wine inside the cage and carefully laid it as a trap to catch me. Presently I appeared, carried by my servants, and came up to the cage, slipping down from my seat to see what they had brought. All I remember is sipping the wine for I must have fallen asleep. Immediately 'Affān shut the cage door and he and Balūqya picked up the cage and headed in the direction of the herb mountain.
'When I eventually awoke from my deep sleep I was very upset to find myself imprisoned in a cage. "Is this the reward of those who do not know the ways of the sons of Ādam?" I said sadly.
'Balūqya answered me gently, explaining that they had come to find the special herb and he assured me that no harm would come to me.

'As soon as we reached the herb mountain the plants that we passed began to speak to us, explaining their properties. After a while a herb spoke up loudly and said that it was the one they were looking for. 'Affān and Balūqya knelt down and picked some leaves, then crushed and squeezed them. Some of the juice they rubbed on their feet and the rest they stored in bottles to take with them. Then they took me back home and set me free.
'I asked the men what they intended to do next and they told me that their plan was to sail the Seven Seas to find King Sulaymān's tomb and to take away his ring.
' "God intended the ring for Sulaymān alone–you will not be able to take it away," I had to tell them. "If you had picked the herb that guarantees to all those who eat it immortality until the first blast of the Trumpet on the Day of Judgement, you might have had a better chance. But this herb you went to so much trouble to get will not help you achieve your purpose."
'The two men were so disappointed that they just turned and walked away from me. I slithered off to search for my band of serpents, only to find that they had become quite wild while I was away. They were overjoyed to see me, however, and after we had exchanged our news we set off for Mount Qāf where we usually spend our winters.'

Hāsib listened fascinated to the Queen of the Serpents' story but by now he was beginning to feel restless and he asked the queen if one of her servants would take him back to the surface of the earth so that he might return to his own people.
'You must wait until winter has come, Hāsib,' replied the queen. 'Then you must come with us to Mount Qāf so that you can see its wondrous slopes, the trees and birds glorifying God there and the jinns and mārids who inhabit its hilly lands and hollow lands.'

Hāsib was disappointed but since there was nothing he could do, he asked her to continue her story of 'Affān and Balūqya.

When the two men left the Queen of the Serpents, they decided to go ahead with their plan anyway. They rubbed some more juice into the soles of their feet and travelled across the

out a mighty blast of flame which almost set the whole cavern on fire, and cried, 'Woe unto you! If you do not leave I shall consume you utterly.'

Balūqya turned and fled from the cavern, but 'Affān bravely continued to advance towards the dead king. Just as he was drawing the ring off Sulaymān's finger, the python blew another mighty blast of fire and within a second, 'Affān was reduced to ashes. Balūqya, who saw what happened from the cavern mouth, was so horrified that he fell down in a faint.

God was merciful to Balūqya and he sent the Archangel Jibrīl to earth to save him. As Balūqya regained consciousness, he saw the Archangel standing beside him. 'Who are you and where did you come from?' asked the archangel. So Balūqya told his story once again. 'I only decided to come here to find the water of life so that I might become immortal and live to see the coming of Muhammad,' he said. 'Please can you tell me where I may find him?' 'Go on your way, Balūqya,' said the Archangel, 'for the time of Muhammad has not yet come.' With those words, Jibrīl went back to heaven, leaving Balūqya distressed and consumed by regret, especially when he remembered the Queen of the Serpent's warning.

Sadly, Balūqya climbed down the mountain and walked towards the shore, where he rubbed some more juice onto his feet and set off across the surface of the sea. At length he reached a fair island that seemed to him like paradise. As he explored, he saw that the soil was saffron, the gravel precious stones; its reeds were sugar canes and its brushwood aloes wood. Birds of every kind sang in gardens of roses, narcissi, white lilies, violets and carnations; gazelles gambolled without fear and wild cattle roamed freely. Balūqya was so entranced by the sight that he lost his way. He walked until it was dark then decided to climb a tree to spend the night. He lay down in its branches, unable to sleep, still wondering at what he had seen.

After a while, the sea began to foam and churn and out of the waves rose a great sea-beast, whose howls made the animals tremble with fear. He was followed by myriads of multi-coloured creatures each carrying a bright jewel which shone like a lamp. Soon the whole of the

Seven Seas. When they reached the shores of the seventh sea, they saw a mountain in the distance whose rocks were emeralds and whose dust was musk. Within a hollow in the mountain they came across a spring of running water which they took as a sign that they were near the end of their journey. Beyond this mountain they came to another, within which was a huge cavern covered by a great shining dome. They climbed up to the cavern and went inside. There they found King Sulaymān, lying on a throne of gold, dressed in green silk embroidered with gold and precious stones. On the middle finger of his hand they saw his ring shining with a light that made all the other jewels in the cavern look dull. 'Affān asked Balūqya to recite incantations and spells while he tried to take off the ring. However, as 'Affān approached the throne a great python slid out from underneath.
'Begone or I will kill you,' it shrieked in a terrible voice, a shower of sparks flying from its mouth. The whole mountain shook and trembled but Balūqya continued to recite the incantations 'Affān had taught him. Then the python blew

shore glowed and shimmered as though basking in sunshine. Presently the sea-beasts were joined by all the panthers, lions and tigers of the island. They spent all night on the shore talking and when day broke they returned to their homes.

In the morning Balūqya decided it was time to leave, so he again applied some of the magic juice and walked on the water, pausing to rest on the islands that separated each of the Seven Seas. After he had crossed five seas he came to another marvellous island. The very soil sparkled like crystal and the flowers on the trees shone like gold. Balūqya walked onto the shore and wandered about until nightfall when the flowers seemed to glow like stars. They made him think that he had stumbled across the kind of flowers which when dried by the sun and swept by the wind under the rocks, turn into the elixir, the substance that turns base metals into gold.

The next morning Balūqya set off across the sixth sea to another island. Here he discovered many more strange and wonderful sights: trees blazing as though on fire, trees with fruit in the shape of human heads hanging by the hair and others with fruit that laughed and wept. Again, when night came, he climbed a tree and settled down to rest for the night. Shortly after dark he woke to the sound of the churning, foaming sea but this time he saw the daughters of the sea walk to the shore, each holding a shining jewel. All night he listened to them singing and dancing around the trees. In the morning they returned to the sea and Balūqya once more applied the magic juice to his feet and set off across the water.

Balūqya travelled across the seventh sea for two months without sighting land. He had no food during that time except raw fish, so he welcomed the sight of an island on which he could see many trees and streams. He walked onto the shore and made for the first apple tree. He was on the point of picking an apple when he heard a voice cry, 'If you eat from the fruit of this tree I will cut you into two halves.'

Balūqya looked up to see a giant figure looming above him. 'Why do you forbid me to eat from this tree?' he asked.

'Because you are a son of Ādam. Ādam broke his faith with God and ate from the forbidden tree,' replied the giant.

'Who are you, what is your name, and to whom does this island belong?' asked Balūqya.

The giant told him that his name was Sharāhya and that he was a guard for King Sakhr. Then, after he had offered Balūqya some food, he listened to his strange story.

The next day, Balūqya said goodbye to the giant and set off inland over sandy deserts and rocky mountains. On the tenth day, he saw a great cloud of dust in the distance. As he walked on, the sound of battle reached him. Drawing nearer he could distinguish two armies fighting but when they saw Balūqya, they all stopped and rode towards him. One of the horsemen came up to him and asked him who he was and where he came from.

'I am one of the sons of Ādam and I have wandered here for the love of Muhammad,' Balūqya told him.

'We have never seen a son of Ādam before,' the horseman said in wonder. 'We are jinns who live in the White Lands and every year we come here to fight the jinns who do not believe in God.'

'Where are the White Lands?' Balūqya asked the knight.

'They lie beyond Mount Qāf, about seventy-five years' distance from here. This country is known as the land of Shaddād, the son of 'Ād. We are fighting on behalf of our king, Sakhr, whom you must come and meet.'

So Balūqya went with the knights to meet their king in the White Lands. When they arrived, Balūqya saw a magnificent pavilion made of red satin, with pegs of gold and silver, surrounded by other tents of green silk. He was led into the red tent to meet King Sakhr who greeted him warmly, and asked him how he came to be so far from home. Balūqya once more told his story while the king listened in wonder. Then food and drink were brought in and the king and his retainers praised the name of God and asked His blessing on Muhammad. Balūqya was surprised to hear the Prophet's name mentioned and asked how they knew about Muhammad. The king started to explain, first giving an account of hell.

'God made hell in seven layers,' he said to

Balūqya. 'Each layer is separated from the others by a distance of a one thousand years' journey. The first layer is called Jahannam and is assigned to the punishment of believers who sin and die unrepentant.'

'There cannot be many tortures in the uppermost layer of hell,' put in Balūqya.

'No, indeed not, but it still contains a thousand mountains of fire, each with seventy-thousand valleys of fire, each with seventy-thousand castles of fire. Each castle contains seventy-thousand houses of fire, each house seventy-thousand couches, and each of these holds seventy-thousand methods of torture. But the torment in this hell is indeed nothing compared to the others.'

Balūqya was so alarmed by this account that he nearly fainted. The king reassured him, 'Fear not, Balūqya, for those who love Muhammad will not burn. As for us, we are made of fire itself.' Then he went on to say that he and his people were the descendants of the first two inhabitants of hell and that they were believers who never ceased praising God.

By now Balūqya was feeling restless and anxious to be on his way so he asked the king for permission to leave, and begged him to ask one of his attendants to take him home.

'We cannot do anything without God's permission. However, if you really wish to leave,' said the king 'allow me to lend you one of my mares. She will take you to the borders of my country where you will meet the men of another king, Barākhya. They will recognize the mare and help you to dismount. Then send the mare back to me.'

Balūqya took his leave and rode the king's mare to the border of King Barākhya's country. There he was taken to see the king, who asked him when he had last seen King Sakhr.

'Two days ago,' replied Balūqya.

'Do you know how many days' journey you have covered in those two days?' asked the king. 'You have covered seventy months.' Balūqya was very surprised to hear this and at the king's invitation he stayed a further two months, during which time he told the story of his quest and adventures once again.

The Queen of the Serpents paused in her long story and Hāsib seized the opportunity to beg her again to help him back to the surface of the earth so that he might return to his family.

'As soon as you have finished greeting your family you will want to go to the public bath, the hammām, to bathe. Then the judgement of God will be upon me because that will be the cause of my death,' the queen told Hāsib.

Hāsib swore that he would never even go near the public bath as long as he lived, and promised to bathe only at home.

'Even if you swore a thousand times, I would not believe you,' replied the queen, 'for you are a son of Ādam and therefore cannot be trusted. Your father broke his covenant with the Lord even though He made the angels bow down before him.'

Saddened by her words, Hāsib held his peace for ten days. Then he went back to the queen and asked her to tell him the rest of Balūqya's adventures.

At last Balūqya took his leave of King Barākhya and set off once more across the desert

and empty wastes until he came to a high mountain. On top of the mountain sat an angel praising God. He had two enormous outspread wings, one to the west and one to the east and in his hand he held a tablet.

'My name is Mikā'il,' the angel told Balūqya, after they had greeted one another. 'I have been given the task of alternating day and night until the Day of Judgement.'

Very much impressed, Balūqya left the angel and resumed his journey. Next he came to a vast calm meadow where four angels knelt under a gigantic tree. As he drew near he saw that one of the angels had the form of a human, another that of a beast, another that of a bird and the last that of a bull. 'O God, I entreat you to forgive all those creatures who are created in my likeness,' they each prayed.

Leaving the four angels in prayer, Balūqya travelled onwards until he at last reached Mount Qāf. There, too, he found an angel seated in prayer but this one, Balūqya noticed, continually opened and closed his hands, bending and stretching his fingers.

After they had exchanged greetings, Balūqya asked, 'Who are you and what do you do on this mountain?'

'This is the mountain of Qāf which encompasses the world,' the angel replied. 'In my hands I hold the reins of all the countries of the earth. Whenever God wishes to cause a great event on earth, an earthquake or a drought, a great peace or plenty, He orders me to fulfill His commands. This I can do without moving from my place, for from here I can control the world.'

Balūqya took his leave of the angel and travelled westwards until he arrived at a great closed gate guarded by two creatures, one like a lion, the other like a bull.

'Who are you? Where have you come from and where are you going' they demanded. 'I am a son of Ādam,' Balūqya replied. 'I have left my own country and have travelled far and wide for the love of Muhammad. But alas I have lost my way. Please tell me who you are and what lies behind that gate.'

'We are the keepers of the gate. Apart from that we have no other task except to praise God,' they told him.

'What is beyond the gate?' asked Balūqya again, overcome by curiosity.

'We do not know,' they answered.

'In the name of God, open it so that I may see for myself,' said Balūqya.

'We cannot open the gate. No-one on earth can open it except Jibrīl the Faithful,' they replied. Balūqya prayed to God to send down Jibrīl to open the gate for him. The Lord listened to his prayer and sent Jibrīl down to open the gate, which was called the Gate of the Meeting of the Two Seas. As soon as the gate was opened, Balūqya stepped in and Jibrīl, locking the gate behind him, ascended back to heaven. Balūqya gazed at the scene that spread magnificently before him. He saw a vast sea whose waters were half salt and half freshwater. On either side rose two mountains of red ruby and by the side of the mountains a host of angels stood worshipping God. When Balūqya asked them about the sea and the two mountains they told him, 'This region lies directly underneath the Throne of God. As for this sea, it feeds all the oceans of the world. Our task is to divide the waters of the sea and send them to the various parts of the earth, the salt water to the salt seas and the freshwater to lakes and rivers. And as for the two mountains they were made by God to guard the waters of the sea until the day of judgement.'

In return Balūqya told his own adventures to the angels and, having finished his story, asked them to show him the way. They pointed to the sea so he rubbed his feet with some of the remaining herb juice and walked on the surface of the water. As he was travelling he made out the huge figures of four angels travelling over the water with the speed of lightning. He called out to them, asking them who they were and where they were going.

'We are the four archangels on our way to do God's bidding. In the east, a terrible serpent has devastated one thousand cities, devouring their inhabitants. We have been ordered to capture it and hurl it down to hell.'

Overwhelmed by the angels' magnitude, Balūqya continued on his journey across the sea until he reached an island where he could see running streams and rich vegetation. He stepped onto the shore to explore. On one tree he saw a

dazzling bird, whose feathers were of precious metals and whose body was of pearls and emeralds. It was praising and singing to the Lord.

'Who are you?' asked Balūqya reverently, 'and what do you do?'

'I am one of the birds of paradise,' answered the bird. I followed Ādam when he was banished from the garden. With Ādam, God cast out four leaves to cover his nakedness and on earth these leaves fell to the ground. One was eaten by worms and from it came silk; another was eaten by gazelles and from it came musk; the third was eaten by bees and so we have honey and the fourth fell in India and so we have spices. I wandered from place to place until God guided me to this island at last and I settled here. Every Friday the saints and holy men from the world come here to eat from this table provided by God for his guests. They stay for one day and one night and then the table is lifted back to paradise.'

Balūqya went over to the table and helped himself to food and then offered his thanks to God. Suddenly he noticed someone walking towards him so he stood up and greeted him. Balūqya was about to leave the table to the stranger but, 'Sit down, Balūqya,' said the bird. 'This is the Prophet Al-Khidr, the Green One,

who has drunk from the waters of immortality.'

Balūqya sat down again, his head bowed in reverence and, at Al-Khidr's request, he retold his adventures from the very beginning. At the end he asked, 'My Lord, tell me how long it will take me to journey back to Egypt?'

'Ninety-five years,' replied Al-Khidr.

Balūqya wept at this news, then went over to Al-Khidr, knelt at his feet and kissed his hand. 'I am nearly dead with fatigue and do not know which way to turn for help. Surely God will reward you if you help me find my way back and release me from my wanderings.' entreated Balūqya.

'Pray to God to permit me to take you back to Egypt,' advised Al-Khidr.

Balūqya implored God to grant him his wish. After a while Al-Khidr told him that God had listened to his prayers and asked him to close his eyes and take hold of him. He took Balūqya by the hand and stepped forward.

'Open your eyes,' he said to Balūqya, who did as he was told, then stood speechless, unable to believe his eyes: in front of him was his own palace. He turned to thank Al-Khidr but the prophet had vanished. Still hardly able to believe his eyes, Balūqya walked through the gate to be greeted warmly by his family and court. There were great celebrations that night for Balūqya was just as pleased to be home as his people were to welcome him.

'So,' concluded the Queen of the Serpents, 'although Balūqya did not realize his ambition to meet Muhammad, he did achieve peace of mind because his journey had helped him to find faith.'

Tears filled Hāsib's eyes as he listened to the ending of the queen's story for it reminded him of his own longing to be home with his mother and his people. Once more he begged the Queen of the Serpents to release him but still she would not trust him to keep his promise. This time, however, he persisted and in the end she gave in to his wishes to go back to the surface of the earth. She sent one of her servants with him as a guide and, after a journey through long dark passages, they came to the mouth of an abandoned well. There the servant left him.

Hāsib hurried back to his mother's house. The

woodcutters had told his mother that he had been devoured by a wolf, so she was both surprised and overjoyed to see him. The woodcutters, however, were very uneasy when they heard of Hāsib's return and sent him presents to try to regain his favour. Afterwards they consulted with merchants of the city who advised them to give Hāsib half of their money and property as compensation. Hāsib forgave the woodcutters and, because of his new found prosperity, the merchants competed with one another to entertain him and win his friendship.

One morning Hāsib was out walking when he met the owner of the public bath. He was at once invited to go into the bath but, greatly worried, declined firmly and told the proprietor that he had taken an oath never to bathe in public. The man insisted and in his turn also swore a binding oath. Hāsib still refused. Eventually their argument attracted the attention of passers-by, who pleaded with Hāsib to go to the bath so as not to cause an innocent man to break his oath. As Hāsib continued to refuse they took him by force and began to undress him. They were just about to pour water over him when twenty men broke in saying that the king was looking for Hāsib. The king's wazīr then appeared with a horse to take Hāsib back to the palace and they all rode off together. The wazīr gave Hāsib food and drink before explaining why they had brought him there. 'Our king lies nearly dead from leprosy, Hāsib, and we have read that his life depends on you.'

The wazīr took Hāsib to see the king, who was a mighty and powerful man, served by many princes and generals. Yet when Hāsib entered the room, expecting to see the king in all his majesty, he saw only a sick man lying on a bed, his face smothered in bandages and obviously in great pain.
'We wish you to cure our king,' said the wazīr.
'But how can I cure him when I know nothing about medicine?' asked Hāsib, perplexed.
'You know the remedy for his illness, for it is none other than the Queen of the Serpents,' said the wazīr.

Alarmed, Hāsib spoke without thinking.
'I do not know the Queen of the Serpents. I have never heard of her before.'

'Ah, but you do,' replied the wazīr. 'I have read in my books that the Queen of the Serpents will meet a man who will stay two years in her company, then return to the surface of the earth. When the man goes to the public bath, his stomach will turn black. Let us look at your stomach, Hāsib.'
'I have always been this colour,' replied Hāsib, looking at his stomach and discovering the truth of the wazīr's words.
'I have had men stationed outside the public baths for some time,' said the wazīr, 'so that I could find a man with a black stomach. You must lead us to the Queen of the Serpents.'

Hāsib was filled with remorse at what he had done and he refused to help the wazīr. Even though Hāsib was beaten until he nearly died, he still would not co-operate.
'Just point the way to her palace,' the wazīr tried to persuade him again, this time gently, 'and no harm will come to you.' Then he showered Hāsib with presents and compliments until at last Hāsib's will was broken and he agreed to take the wazīr to the place where he had emerged from the other world.

With a heavy heart, Hāsib led the wazīr to the well. There the wazīr sat burning incense and reciting spells until there was a tremendous noise, followed by sounds of weeping and lamentations. The lid of the well lifted and a giant serpent with eyes like burning coals appeared. On her back she carried a tray on which was seated a serpent with a human head and voice, shining with a glowing light. The Queen of the Serpents looked to the right and to the left until her eyes fell on Hāsib.
'What became of the oath you swore to me and of all those promises you made? But it is no use fighting against fate, for God has ordained that you will be the cause of my death. It is His will that I should die that the king may be healed.'

The wazīr stepped forward to catch the serpent, but she was too quick for him and hissed at him, threatening to reduce him to ashes. She called to Hāsib and asked him to carry her and her tray on his head.
'You shall walk with me for it is written that my death will be on your hands and we cannot avoid our fates.'

As they made their way to the palace, the Queen of the Serpents whispered to Hāsib: 'Listen to what I say and do whatever I tell you for inspite of your betrayal I will give you good advice. When we arrive at the palace, the wazīr will order you to kill me and to cut me into three parts. You must refuse, pretending that you do not know how to do such a thing and let him do the killing himself. When he has killed and divided me, a messenger will come from the king asking for the wazīr. Before leaving he will lay me in a copper cauldron and place it upon the fire. Then he will say this to you: "Tend the fire carefully and watch for the first froth that rises to the surface. As soon as it forms, skim it off and pour it into a bottle. When it has cooled, you must drink it for it will cure your body of every pain and disease. Then wait until the second froth forms. Skim this off too and pour it into this bottle. Keep it carefully until I return for it will cure me of a pain in my back".'

The Queen of the Serpents lowered her voice still more so that Hāsib could scarcely hear her soft hissing whisper. 'Whatever you do, do not drink from that first bottle for it will cause you great harm. Drink instead from the second bottle for its contents will give you wisdom. When the wazīr comes back give *him* the first bottle to drink and see what will happen! As for my flesh, when it is cooked, take it out and lay it on a copper plate. Give it to the king to eat, then cover his face with a towel. Leave him like this until noon, then give him something to drink but leave his face covered for three days. When you uncover it again after this time you will find him completely cured, in perfect health and strength.'

Everything happened as the Queen of the Serpents had predicted. As soon as the first froth formed, Hāsib poured it into a bottle and put it on one side. With eyes still wet from mourning the dead queen, he skimmed the second froth and waited for the wazīr to return.

Eventually the wazīr appeared. 'Did you drink the first froth?' he asked.
'Indeed sir, I obeyed my instructions,' replied Hāsib carefully. 'Then give me the bottle that remains,' said the wazīr eagerly, almost snatching it from Hāsib. He drank it in a single gulp.

The wazīr had hardly finished drinking when the bottle dropped from his grasp. His body began to swell and in a moment he fell to the ground, dead. At first Hāsib was too frightened to drink from the second bottle himself but, remembering the Queen of the Serpent's words, he put his trust in God and took a cautious sip. At once he was filled with a feeling of ecstasy and a great fountain of knowledge seemed to flow into his mind. He finished the bottle eagerly, then laid the flesh of the dead serpent on a copper plate and carried it away to the king's chamber.

As he passed through the courtyards, he looked up at the sky and there revealed to him were the seven heavens and the blessed Tree of the Ultimate. He saw the spheres revolving and understood the movements of the planets and the position of the fixed stars. He knew the contours of the land and the depths of the sea and understood the arts of astrology, astronomy, geometry and mathematics. Then he looked into the earth and discovered all that it contains of minerals and vegetation; he could see clearly their properties and uses and knew as if by instinct the arts of medicine, alchemy and magic and the making of gold and silver.

When Hāsib reached the king's chamber he was admitted instantly. He explained that the wazīr had died and asked the king to eat the meat he had brought with him. Then, as the Queen of the Serpents had ordered, he covered the king's face with a towel and left him. After three days the king was completely recovered; the disease had left him without a trace and he was restored to perfect health.

The king was so impressed by this miracle of healing that he appointed Hāsib his new wazīr and rewarded him lavishly. Hāsib's wisdom and knowledge became famous throughout the land. One day he asked his mother about his inheritance from his father and she gave him the five pages and told him how she had kept them all these years. Hāsib read the pages and understood them well. Then he placed them carefully in a casket and thanked God for the gifts of wisdom and wealth that had transformed his meaningless existence into a rich and purposeful life.

Symbols in the Arabic myths and legends

At the beginning of each chapter the artist has illustrated some of the symbols and characters from the stories.

p.11 THE ARABS AND THEIR WORLD Incense made from the gum and resin of the frankincense tree *(Boswellia thurifera)* was one of the most important trade goods of the ancient world and was used in all religious ceremonies. The bushes were cultivated along the southern coastlands of Arabia and in the colonies of Somalia and Socotra. Below, camels are perfectly adapted to desert conditions and were fundamental to the desert Arabian's way of life. They provided milk, meat, transport, tents (from hides) and even clothing.

p. 16 GODS OF THE ANCIENT ARABS Top: The Ka'ba or Sacred House at Mecca, the centre of the Islamic world. Below: The sacred Well of Zamzam sprang from the ground at Izm'āil's feet; golden gazelles were among the idols worshipped within the Sacred House by pagan Arabs. Bottom: The legend of Nūh (Noah) and his ark is common to both ancient Arab and Hebrew tradition. A recent theory is that the ark would have been made from reeds, like the ancient reed boats of the area.

p.32 MYTHS AND LEGENDS OF THE EXTINCT ARABS The remains of ancient rock-built cities such as Petra inspired many of the myths dealing with lost civilizations. Centre, kohl, a thick black powder used to outline the eyes, has been used for thousands of years. In this chapter its origin is explained. Below, the giant 'Ād, great-great grandchild of Sām.

p.49 MYTHS AND LEGENDS OF THE NORTH AND SOUTH The ancient desert kingdoms of the North contrasted with the lush groves and gardens of the kingdom of Saba (Sheba), made possible by the irrigation schemes of Ma'rib.

p.68 PRIESTS, SOOTHSAYERS AND WISE MEN The fable of the wind and the sun (top) and of the hen that laid a silver egg (bottom) are well known outside the Arab world through the writing of the Greek Aesop. Centre: Soothsayers foretold the future or interpreted mysterious events by 'reading' the patterns of cast stones, cowrie shells or grains of wheat.

p.77 TALES OF GENEROSITY, HONOUR AND LOYALTY Top: A pattern taken from Bedouin beadwork frames a portrait of Mawiyya, the wife of Hātim, most generous of Arabs. Hātim's generosity (symbolized by the camels) and hospitality (here, roasting meat) were outstanding examples of the desert Arabs' code of honour.

p.87 CELESTIAL AND TERRESTRIAL WORLDS The Sun and Moon (partly, darkened by an angel's wing) with planets and stars. Below, vapour rising from the water to form the sky.

p.95 ANGELS AND JINN The angel Isrāfil within whose trumpet the souls of the dead were thought to be kept until the Day of Judgement. Below are an angel in the form of a falcon, and the two lances of the Angel of Death. Bottom: The race of jinn, formed from smokeless fire, come below the angels in the celestial heirarchy.

p.103 THE ARABIAN NIGHTS The cockerel (top) symbolizes the passing of another night, granting another day of life to Sharazad. Below are scenes and characters from the vast collection of tales she told.

p.108 THE CITY OF BRASS The minarets and domes of the mysterious City with, below, the ships which carried the travellers to the place where jinn were realeased from their sealed vessels (bottom). The story starts as a quest to find the jinn but like many of the stories in the Arabian Nights, becomes a story within a story as the journey progresses. This tradition of complex story-telling helped Sharazād to keep the king in suspense from night to night.

p.117 JOURNEYS TO THE WORLD OF THE SUPERNATURAL Top, Hāsib encounters the Queen of the Serpents, whose story is interwoven with his own and with Baluqya's quest for enlightenment.

Sources

Al-'Alūsi, Mahmūd, *Balugh Al-'Irab*, *(Achievement of Purpose)*, (Cairo 1934).

Al-'Aghāni, S., *Arab Fairs: Jāhiliyyah and Islām*, (Damascus, 1960).

Al-'Asbahānī, *Al-'Aghānī*, *(Book of Songs)*, (Leiden, 1900).

Al-Daynūrī, *Al'-Akhbār Al-Tiwāl (The Long Chronicles)*, (Cairo, 1960).

Al-Hamadānī, *Al-'Iklīl (The Crown)*, (Baghdad, 1931).

Al-Hūt, M. Salim, *Mythology and the Arabs*, Beirut, 1955).

Al-Mas'ūdī, *Murūj Al-Dhahab (Golden Meadows)*, (Beirut, 1981).

Al-Mawla, M.A.J., *Stories of the Koran*, (Damascus, 1981).
  Stories of the Arabs, (Cairo, 1971).

Al-Mīdānī, *Majama' Al'-Amthāl (Collected Proverbs)* Beirut, 1955).

Al-Qazwīnī, *'Aja'ib Al-Makklūqāt (Wonders of Creation)*, (Beirut, 1981).

Al-Shiblī, *Akām Al-Murjān fi Ahkām Al-Jān (The Jinn)*, (Cairo 1908).

Al-Tabarī, *Tārikh Al-Rusul wa l-Mulūk (History of Prophets and Kings)*, (Leiden, 1884).

Al-Ya'qūbī, *Tārikh Al-ya'qūbī (History of Al-Ya'qūbī)*, (Leiden, 1883)

Al-Sha'bī, *Kitab Siyar Al-Mulūk (Lives of Kings)*, British Museum (Add 18,505).

Al-Tha'labī, *Qisas Al-'anbiyā (Stories of Prophets)*, (Cairo, 1859).

'Aql, Nabīh, *Ancient History of the Arabs*, (Damascus, 1975).

Burton, R.F. *Thousand Nights and One*, Benares, 1885).

Dayf, Shawqī, *Al-Jāhiliyyah Period*, (Cairo, 1976).

Doughty, C.M. *Travels in Arabia Deserta*, (London, 1930)

Gabrieli, G., *Arab Islamic Bibliography* eds. Grimwood-Jones, D., Hopwood, D., and Pearson, J.D. (Harvesters Press, 1972).

Gerhardt M.I. *The Art of Story-Telling*, 1963

Gibb, H.A.R., Kramers, J.H., and Schacht, J. (eds), *Encyclopaedia of Islam*, (London 1960).

Hitti, P. *History of the Arabs*, (London, 1956).

Holt, P.M., Lambton, A.S., and Lewis, B. (eds). *The Cambridge History of Islam*, (Cambridge 1970).

Ibn Al-'Athīr, *Al-Kāmil fi l-Tārikh (The Complete in History)*, (Leiden, 1899).

Ibn Al-Kalbī, *Al-'Asnām (Book of Idols)*, trans. Nabīh Amīn Fāris, (New Jersey, 1952).

Ibn Batūtah, *Travels of Ibn Batūtah*, (Beirut, 1981).

Ibn Kāthīr, *Al-Bidāyah wa l-Nihāyah (The Beginning and the End)*, (Cairo, 1932).

Ibn Khaldūn, *All-Muqaddimah (The Preface)*, (Cairo, 1930).

Ibrāhīm Iskandar, *Mythological Thinking in Arab History*, (Cairo, 1962).

Ikhwān Al-Safā, *The Epistles of the Brethren of Serenity*, (Beirut, 1957).

Tuhfat Ikhwān Al-Safā, British Museum (Add 23467).

Khān, M. Abd Al-Muʿīn *Arab Myths before Islam*, (Cairo, 1937).

Lane, E.W. *Manners and Customs of the Modern Egyptians*, (London, 1954).

Lukman, *Lukman's Arabic Fables*, trans. Francis Barham, (Bath, 1869).

Nicholson, R.A., *A Literary History of the Arabs*, (Cambridge, 1930).

The Arabian Nights, editions (London, 1853), (Bulaq, 1862)

Index

How to pronounce the names

In order to help you to pronounce the names in this book, we have included various symbols and combinations of letters to represent Arabic sounds. These are:

VOWELS

a　as in *at*
ā　as in *aa*h
u　as in p*u*t
ū　as in m*oo*n
i　as in s*ee*n
ay　as in tr*y*
au　as in n*ow*

CONSONANTS

th　as in *th*ree
dh　as in *th*e
kh　as in the Scottish lo*ch*
gh　as in the French me*r*ci

'　glottal stop. This is a catch at the back of the throat. In the middle of a word it occurs as a pause between syllables. If you say 'oh, oh' with a clear break between each one you have a sound resembling a glottal stop.

'　this is a guttural sound which has no equivalent in English. It is made by contracting the throat and expelling air.